Dedication

For Joan, with whom I sailed
the unknown seas without fear

Author's Note

The journey is a true account of all that happened. Only the names of the people with whom I shared the journey have been fabricated in order to protect their identities. The strange and paranormal happened just as I have reported them; I cannot lie or embellish the truth, as this would mock the essence of my purpose: to share with you a realm beyond imagination, which is and has been my reality since I was born. Sometimes it takes a leap of trust to understand the incredible. I am not asking you to take a leap, or even a jump—just a few small steps with me into the Land of Colour, where I danced in the rain with blue feet!

Chapters

1

Yesterday's York

Cold, moist air cloys my nostrils. I shiver. Damp clings to my hair like a limp, lank rag. A boy barks through the mist, coughing roughly, while the early morning wears a lid, sealing white vapour inside the city walls. I walk. Faces pass dreamily through the early morning fog as I glimpse the familiar carved pale stone of the imposing Minster. York, a place where shadows from the past linger and haunt the few who see. Down the years, I have glimpsed many strange entities suspended in a twilight zone, locked in a time warp of their own making, crying, unheard through the ancient bricks.

I slip by Dean's Corner, the windiest spot in the city, but today it is not; only the fog curls mysteriously, clouding the famous Rose Window. The eerie silence stirs secret images of the Lost Roman Legion who marched through the Minster crypt walls, floating in limbo searching for sanctuary. Through the impenetrably cloudy veil, they pass unnoticed with fixed, glazed eyes staring ahead under their shiny helmets.

Memories tumble from my brain. I am estranged from them. I hear my little daughter's voice from the past, "My sisters go to school with the big Minster . . ." I smile, but it is painful to remember. Black iron railings protrude near the single Roman column left standing incongruously by the Song School. Red House, my children's preparatory school, jeers with false welcome. It was friendly before my divorce, and then when I couldn't afford it, the ladies in their fine hats stopped speaking to me. The Minster still looms beside me and, alone in the haze, I am closer to myself, nearer to the person I was somewhere in the past. Was she really "Yorkshire's Voice of Health and Fitness"? I buried her a long time ago. Strangers no longer stop me in the street with their health problems or enquiries about how to make the most of their breasts! I am anonymous as I weave my way down the Shambles, where once the blood-red cobbles smelt of freshly butchered meat, slop, sewage, and rotting vegetables.

The sun struggles to smile, cutting through the impacted cloud above the tiny medieval attic windows and resting briefly for a moment on Saint Margaret Clitheroe's shrine. Already, a few American visitors gather to hear her sad story, but the rays disappear and the mist returns, whispering softly, disguising the dawn traders' calls from the market. Early morning belongs to the vendors, the traders, the packers and unpackers, the beggars with their dogs and blankets, the elderly early risers, the school-children, and the office workers, yet the streets are surprisingly quiet, wrapped in a cotton-wool mantle. It is a time of respect before the curtain rises on the day and the morning unfolds with the shoppers, the visitors, the tourists, and the commerce wizards who infest the streets with their mobiles and techno-logical gadgets that echo off the Roman columns past the river where the fog lurks, thickly confusing the past with the present, where my memories are locked in the bricks and the fabric of the streets. I cannot sidestep them. The medieval city walls encase my past, and part of me is trapped inside forever. There are shades of yesterday everywhere. I trace them forlornly. My children have gone. I realize that Yesterday's York was then, and now I am nearing my destination. The mist lifts, and I see that I have already walked halfway into tomorrow as the now encom-passes all.

The past ten years of flying across Europe; dancing through the Mediterranean; soaking up the energy of live performances, empowered with weighty responsibility, makes the now uneasy. I pine to be back in the sunshine, twirling my way across Europe, not pacing a pathway through the September mist to classroom warfare. Ten years' absence from mainstream teaching has left a gaping hole in my tolerance levels. The rules have changed, making it hard for the teacher to teach without solid sanctions to back up discipline problems. I am not prepared to compromise my principles for the sake of an easy life.

"Hey teacher, leave those kids alone . . ." hangs jauntily in the air, as the song from the past drifts from a nearby music store and, all in all, it's just another brick in the wall from yesterday.

I accept my situation. The sun streaks mischievously across my path as I descend the stone steps by the river, passing the famous Richard the Third Pub, waterlogged so many times that the stone flag floor remains in a state of half repair. Visitors flock to see how high the flood water rises each year and marvel at the building's resilience. I marvel at my own as I struggle to rebuild my life once again. I had given up my high-powered job to settle down in a beautiful old cottage on the outskirts of York with a man I thought I loved, but my voices whispered his deceit. I listened one sunny Sunday afternoon while standing in my kitchen. He was ostensibly playing golf, and I let the voices lead me upstairs to one of his suit-jacket pockets, where I found a reservation for two people in a hotel, for a nonsmoking room!

I knew it straight away, and so it had to be, back to the lonely pathway. I'm not complaining! I'm not bitter. I believe in the greater picture. My psychic gift has always taught me that all things are what they need to be. In my "nowness," I know and understand why it had to happen and thank him for helping me to obtain my beautiful cottage, but the mortgage struggle tethers me to the Education battleground, and an ongoing tax investigation hangs over me like a black-hooded thief, watching, waiting, poised to strike! Now the September sunshine showers the River Ouse with spangled sequins, and a profound sense of restlessness broods deep within. I pause for a moment on Ouse Bridge, feeling the need to jump off the edge of routine into the deep waters of uncertainty. I want to escape the monotony that stifles all magical connection with synchronicity. I need to fling open all possibilities of experiencing new adventures. I want to jour-

3

ney where I am nothing, where I know no one, and test myself out in the Universe. I need to be free to explore new territory without the pull or tug of a loved one left behind. Dull domesticity, mingled with fear of failure and a tax burden tortures me. Waking up in the middle of the night with cold panic attacks threatening my existence, my house, my home, my future with nightmare consequences of bankruptcy and, worst of all, the possibility of a prison sentence, I know I must break free.

The water sparkles, and I am reminded of the story of Jesus. I am not religious, but the tale of the "little blue fishes" affords me some comfort, especially as Jesus owed a considerable amount of tax! He knew of little blue fish that dredged gold coins and other bright objects off the sea bed carrying them in their mouths for safekeeping. Jesus used his psychic gift to direct his disciples to fish in the precise spot where they would seize enough to cover the debt. One day I will find my little blue fishes and I will be saved from the cold nightmare.

A chilly breeze sweeps over my face as I continue across the bridge and round the corner to Baile Hill. Memories here belong to my son as a teenager, meeting his friends with a bottle of wine to party at night in the moonlight. Baile Hill, a special place hidden from the public gaze, holds secrets of battles and heroic deaths, now parcelled in a neat nature reserve for the residents, sponsored by the council.

A York tour bus sails by with a handful of autumn visitors cocooned in bright woollen scarves in the open-top double-decker. They appear safe, almost snug in their certainty of tomorrow. I don't want safe routine. I crave adventure. I need to go on an expedition somewhere, somehow. Six weeks during the long summer holidays would be ideal, unseating me from my safe existence, testing my skills of survival. Every journey is a trial and tests the traveller to a greater or lesser degree, so each time you trust yourself to the will of the Universe, the greater the lesson learned, the more valuable the prize, the deeper the insight into the realm between worlds. I need to know myself further, beyond yesterday's tomorrow. As I walk on, the idea settles into my brain, becoming firmly lodged into the possibility of the possible. Walking further on, the possible grows firmly into the probable until all that remains is "when."

Planning and plotting, I reach the shops in Bishopthorpe Road, a place with a haunting memory of my youngest daughter, age two, running into the busy road straight in front of a motorbike, which nearly killed her by a hair's breadth! It was such a long time ago, but I still sigh with relief as I pass the house of tears, a place I am glad to forget. The telephone box, where my eldest daughter was trapped by two delinquent boys who sealed her inside by binding up the box with tape, is still in use, and the fish-and-chip shop, where I bought my son's first supper treat, which ended in disaster when a massive fish bone got lodged in his throat and he had to be rushed to hospital, is still thriving. Bishopthorpe Road is where my second daughter's little friend was run over. I lay in the middle of the road next to her, holding her still, promising her all kinds of things to calm her until the ambulance came. Four children and a head full of memories! I watched them all walk up the school drive wearing the navy uniforms. I now chase their past shadows through the corridors, teaching in their school to be close to them in nostalgia. The school gates are open and a handful of pupils stub out their cigarettes behind the bushes, dispersing guiltily as I pass. "Hey up, Miss, y'all right, Miss?" I smile. I have a new weapon. I am going to escape. I have a goal, a protective armor against the awaiting enemy in the Science block; even when they attempt to kill the fish swimming innocently in the tank and throw a new computer out of the window, I have something to cling to, knowing that yesterday and today will find a new tomorrow.

2

Chasing the Dance

There are dreams and there are dreams; some you easily discard like dandelion seeds in the wind, but the real dreams, the real scenes, remain forever; like the ancient rhymes in odyssey times, you will know 'til the twelfth of never.

—*L.A.Eden*

I have chased the Dance across the world, hiding my psychic and healing gifts behind a professional front of Choreographer and Dancer. I have glided through one aspect of my world as a Teacher, suppressing the real me, concealing my true identity, while striving to maintain normality with four children, two divorces, and countless pets! I have been used as a channel for electric healing energy, which has pulsed through my hands and helped many people, mostly children. My own children have inherited the gifts, applying them in their own spheres, and I take great comfort from this.

I have tracked down lost steps in faraway places, searching out the melody to rekindle the Dance. Through the years, I have known many steps, felt the sway, held the rhythm, tasted the salty sweat in the late-afternoon rains when the hurricane bites, lashing wooden shutters in a fragile Cuban village. I have been petrified by the pink electric storm howling like a jazz singer in a New Orleans oyster bar, and been rocked to sleep on the beach by a soft sea under the distant gaze of the gentle Pyrenees mountain breeze, remembering many other wonderful places that still echo in my mind, while I am locked in a classroom of sighs and yearn to be released. Where have all the years strayed?

The winter term slowly plods, the smell of damp, cold coats suffuses the chilly corridors right into the classroom. The staff room harbours a few snuffly teachers, intermittently coughing and blowing noses, as the dinner lady pours hot water into the coffee cups, the aroma of cardboard coffee granules wafts into the quiet area. My computer is silent, but "Creative Writing in Guatemala" sidles across the screen and waits until I acknowledge it. How did it creep into my documents?

CREATIVE WRITING IN GUATEMALA screams adventure! Excitedly, I follow the trail, working my way through a host of different ideas. I abandon the books I need to mark and give in to the enticement of spending my free period tracking down adventure. One hour later, I have secured my place on an expedition and paid for the airfare, hotels, and tickets! I did not intend to do it, but the little arrow to "click here" seduced me until I had completed the operation. I had never booked anything online before and felt scared, elated, and shocked! I had wanted "Creative Writing in Guatemala" and ended up booking an amazing Mayan adventure!

Six weeks travelling through Central America led by a guide taking a party of strangers through Mexico, Guatemala, Belize, and Antigua and out to a tiny Caribbean island where no cars or roads exist, staying in primitive accommodations, trekking through the rain forest, and exploring the Mayan temples was mind blowing! I had acted spontaneously but began to have doubts about whether I could physically deal with the trip, as my long-term knee injury, through years of dance, left me at a disadvantage for climbing volcanoes and ascending mountainous temple steps.

7

I decided not to think about that and just begin the long preparation for the trip. There was so much to plan and consider besides checking all the necessary injections and health regulations. The organisers had no idea how many would be in the party, but assured me that there would probably be about six or seven people doing the full tour. It was the company's policy to use local transport wherever they could and to double up on accommodations. The idea of sharing a room with someone I didn't like for the full duration of the trip was unnerving, but was part of the adventure!

At the special travel clinic, the nurse advised me of the necessary health precautions, including a self-help travellers' stomach-bug kit and a course of injections for rabies, which would give me a twenty-four-hour chance of survival, if I were bitten by a rabid animal. I was given a series of injections for most diseases, one or two of which were quite painful, and anti-malaria tablets. I hadn't had so much serum injected into me since my first trip to India, but I was younger then and able to cope much better with the poison in my body.

That night, wrapped in the new thrill of anticipation, I lay awake, happy to be alone again, relieved not to share sleeping space or have to pretend emotions. I was free to absorb the silence. I couldn't wait for my journey to begin! Suddenly a searing pain bore its way through my gut. I rolled and reeled across the bed, trying to escape the attack. I was afraid, and being alone suddenly didn't seem so good. The sharp stabs shot me into a different dimension. I thought I had lost the ability to go out beyond the confines of my body, so I strangely welcomed the shock of hanging suspended in a thick, black sphere, floating in abject nothingness. Time drifted, existed, ceased, forever was never, without beginning or end. Time seemed suspended until a purple mist, a swirling cloud of energy, encompassed me and I was sucked into its comforting, healing, all-embracing amethyst mass. Its vibration eased all discomfort, allowing me to slowly drift back.

Gradually I returned back inside my body and managed to haul myself up and drag myself to the bathroom. The moon was a sturdy friend, staring down through the ceiling window. All was calm, the pain diminished, and I slumped back to a chaotic slumber. Through the fever, helping hands of unseen friends prepared me, pushing me out of my comfort zone into the Universe, where I could stand up and say, "Here I am. What now?" and as the light slowly trickled through the blinds, I felt better.

The next day, fully recovered, I lumbered through the dining hall laden with books as the sickly-sweet smell of artificial raspberry jam roly-poly with insipid custard tainted the air. Mutiny hung all around, unseen but felt close at hand, as boys whispered in corners and kicked one another randomly. The end of the Christmas term brought the obligatory rebellious attempts at setting off the fire alarm, and one ingenious person succeeded! Classes noisily spilled out onto the muddy football field, relieved to have unscheduled time out of class. Teachers marched up and down, officiously taking names, while the Deputy Head appeared like a messiah on the top ridge, his long white beard and frail hair quivering in the icy wind. My new black boots squelched in the mud as I shivered in the bleak afternoon. The thought of a far-way adventure spurred me on as I lead my unenthusiastic pupils back into the classroom.

At the weekend, I decided to cheer myself up by buying equipment I would need for the expedition—a heavy-duty backpack, mosquito repellent, a roll-up travel towel, waterproof top, and trousers. I displayed the goods on the kitchen table and admired them, along with a good bottle of red wine I had purchased with the little money I had left over. Cosily sipping the red wine alone on a Saturday night would normally have made me depressed, but now it was a party for one! I was celebrating my newfound independence. The shiraz warmed me as I sat in the kitchen wrapped in my heavy coat. I kept the heat in the house turned way down, as I was afraid of a hefty bill. The fear of the huge tax demand floated above me while I succumbed to the deadening numbness of alcohol. My escape route was planned. I would be free for six weeks! The night closed in, and the music seduced me onto an imaginary dance floor, where I swayed in the arms of a tall, dark stranger. The evening wore away painlessly with hypnotic rhythms . . . dancing . . . dancing . . . .

I survived my first year back at school and was relieved when the term finally came to a halt like a steam train that, having climbed up a very steep hill, puffs its final breath and retires into the station for the night. The sun shone lazily as I collected my books and cleared out my desk; I had one day left to go before I set off for my magical adventure. Waving to the last stragglers out of the school gates, I drove home with excitement churning in my stomach, tinged with fear. The next day was spent checking all my gear and also last-minute shopping in York. As I returned with my bags, awkwardly opening the door with one hand, I was knocked backward as the air was heavy with gas. A gas leak! I was on the verge of a great adventure and I had a domestic crisis! Fighting back tears, I fumbled through the phone book to find the emergency gas number. The leak was coming from the old cooker. My mind reeled with what-ifs. Luckily, the Gas Board was prompt and sent a man out within the hour. I was so thankful to have some support and someone to assure me that all would be well. I shuddered to think that if I had left the house with a leak, I would have been blown up on my return!

I looked at my watch. Three hours to go before I was due to leave, and I had a gas leak? The man worked efficiently and thoroughly, calming my fears, and, after the final all-clear, I was relieved to be out of danger. But there was a new fear ahead. Terrorists had plotted to bomb ten American Airline jets, and my plane to Miami was one of them! Heathrow Airport was in calamitous chaos, with thousands of stranded passengers. I paused in the garden for a while as the late July sun cast light shadows across the lawn. I wondered what the garden would look like on my return. Would my journey change me? Would I even return? I had made a will for my children in case of my death; it seemed a sensible thing to do under the circumstances.

In jeans and black poncho, which I bought in the mountains in Teneriffe, I looked like one of Indiana Jones' sidekicks, albeit incongruously, with sleek, long blonde hair. A chilly wind rustled the grass as I closed the creaky gate and took one last look at the cottage before boarding the taxi to the bus station. It seemed odd, sitting opposite the railway station at six-thirty in the evening waiting for a double-decker to Leeds, travelling so light, without my vanity case, jewellery, evening dresses, and countless changes of clothes.

On arriving at Leeds bus station, I resigned myself to the long four-hour wait with a small bottle of gin and tonic a friend had prepared for me, and surrendered myself to the situation. I became invisible in the waiting area as it metamorphosed into a sitting room for pimps and their prostitutes. The girls fascinated me. They were so sure of their bodies, with their long, olive-skinned legs, immaculate make-up, and beautifully coiffed hair. They lounged across the seats as though they were at home watching television, while their pimps busied themselves arguing on their mobiles in a foreign language to possible punters. One girl wore a sarong tied low at her hip, displaying her inner thigh as she lay across the bench, bending her legs teasingly while painting her toenails. I was entertained by their comings and goings until the bus pulled into the bay.

I boarded and settled into my seat with coffee and sandwiches. I felt snug travelling out into the night watching the slumbering houses veiled by the yellow electric streetlights, deserted except for the moon. I wondered what Heathrow would be like after the major scare and was prepared to face long queues and delays. I managed an intermittent nap, but I was too excited to really sleep. The roads were clear by the time I reached Heathrow, and, in the early hours of the morning, it was quiet, strangely empty like a ghost town, with only a skeleton cleaning staff. Lines of empty trolleys were scattered about, abandoned as if in the aftermath of a holocaust. There was no evidence of the chaos portrayed earlier in the news. As I trundled my trolley along the deserted tunnel, the sound of the wheels reverberated off the walls. I was alone and nervous. I had not expected the deep, hollow echo of isolation, only noise and confusion. A few hours later, crowds infiltrated every breathing space like a swarm of ants on a candy bar. Pandemonium broke

11

out in all directions. I was pushed to the back of a long queue at a different check-in counter, where everyone was handed a clear plastic bag in which to keep their money and passport; everything else had to be placed in the hold of the aircraft. Anarchy and confusion was the rule of the day as everyone clamoured for further advice and clarification of the new rules.

Fearfully, I placed my handbag on the conveyor belt. It contained my world for the next six weeks, so I prayed it wouldn't get stolen and that I would retrieve it safely in Miami. I pushed my way through the mayhem and managed to find a step on the escalator. The hours wait in the overbearing cacophony gave me a headache, and, when I finally boarded the plane, a further two-hour delay ensued while the baggage was unloaded and reloaded in another thorough search for bombs. I fell asleep, missing the take-off and the chance to wave good-bye to England. I was lost in bewilderment and fatigue, travelling backward through the sky to a new world of tomorrow to chase the Dance in a different sphere.

3

Miami Mayhem

The plane was late arriving in Miami, and I was anxious about missing my connecting flight to Mexico. We landed at eleven o'clock in the evening American time, and my connection was scheduled to fly to Cancun at ten-thirty. I was terrified that I would miss my guide. My daughter had informed me that she had read about a group of tourists on a similar expedition who had been murdered in a forest because they didn't have a guide! That fear, along with the idea of being stranded all night in Miami, unnerved me.

Everyone began complaining, muttering in low voices as they alighted from the plane. The process seemed slower than usual, and being at the back made it worse. I struggled to control my rising panic and broke out in a cold sweat. "We apologise for the delay due to the hold-up in London," drawled a high-pitched American woman's voice over the loudspeakers. "All passengers making connections will be met by staff, who will be pleased to advise you . . . "

This gave me some reassurance, but my heart was still pounding. The success of the journey would depend upon meeting the guide safely in Mexico, so this first connection was vital. Stepping out into the humid Miami night was like entering a steamy sauna fully clothed. The airport electrically buzzed bewildered disorder. The runway was jammed with late-arriving planes and overloaded shuttle buses. Hysterical passengers began to run wildly to any available bus in panic, infectiously alarming other passengers, who started pulling and pushing one another out of the way.

No one seemed to be in control. Being small, I found myself squashed up against peoples' chests with my hands pressed against my breasts to protect myself, choked by the smell of stale sweat. The uncomfortable bus ride was only a few short minutes, but it seemed an eternity. As the bus screeched to a halt and the hoard disembarked, my hope for a speedy check-in was dashed.

The massive security checkpoint was fairly heaving with swarms of bodies. Queues upon queues of tired, angry people staled the humid night air. A skeleton staff struggled with the backlog of travellers. Every minute ticking by was torture. I was afraid of being left stranded in the airport. When I finally reached the desk, a young man in front was arguing with the officer over passport problems, and what should have been a mundane routine check-through became a rigorous investigation. I grew resentful toward the young man who was costing me precious time, but when I got to the desk, I found I had not filled in my green card correctly and was sent away to fill in the missing details. Tears of frustration welled as I hurried to a tiny spot on the floor where there was space to write. Anxiously I ran back to the front of the queue, upsetting some English travellers, but there wasn't time to explain my desperate fight against the clock.

Finally with my passport stamped, I dashed out into the corridor like a prisoner let loose from a long hard sentence, only to be thrown into a worse nightmare! Planeloads of passengers were crammed into a cramped walkway, all thrusting forward to get to the check-in desks. No one was on hand to help. A wave of fear washed over me. Sweat dripped off my chin as I clutched my poncho and my little plastic bag containing my money and passport, fending off the army of furious passengers folding in on me.

Suddenly a tsunami of bodies swept backward as people from the front pushed behind. The force sent a hoard of us reeling out of the building into the heat of the night. I lost my poncho, which was trampled underfoot somewhere, but I managed to cling desperately to my plastic bag. I picked myself up off the floor, shocked and shaking with rage as I surged forward, scurrying under the barrier to get back inside. Unfortunately a soldier outside spotted me and gave chase, thinking I was entering the building illegally! I didn't care. It was survival. I darted through a gap in the crowd and ran up the blue-carpeted stairs where an airline official stood directing the stream of bodies. I stood right under his nose and demanded attention. The soldier caught up with me but left when he realised that I was just another lost passenger. The attendant listened to my plight and directed me to a desk where another queue had formed. I began to understand how Alice in Wonderland felt when everything spiralled out of control. Waiting in the queue, hunger pangs began to churn my stomach; I hadn't eaten for hours and my throat was dry. My body ached with fatigue and I could hardly breathe.

Half an hour later, I reached the desk. I was seething with anger. Trembling, with high- pitched voice, I lobbed my complaints at the official but broke down sobbing, not able to contain myself. He was not moved, but informed me politely that there were no more connections that night and I had to wait for another flight in the morning. He did, however, let me have the use of a phone. Embarrassed, I wiped away my tears, fumbling to find the emergency number that I kept in my passport. My mobile was in my handbag, which hopefully had not been stolen and was waiting for me on a carousel somewhere in the airport. The number kept ringing and ringing. There was no reply, not even a chance to leave a message. In desperation I tried to phone my eldest daughter in England, but all I could do was leave a message in the hope that she could contact the tour operator.

Desolate, frightened, and lonely, I made my way to the baggage claim through a sea of angry passengers. I was plagued with doubt about finding my handbag and backpack, and attacked myself with more worry as to what I would do if they were lost. Somehow I managed to find the right area through a maze of corridors and fought my way across a battlefield of bodies, bags, and pushchairs, where, amazingly, I found both my belongings sailing around on the carousel. I snatched my handbag to my chest like a lost child and heaved my backpack quickly onto the floor. At least one major obstacle had been lifted from the list! It was now two o'clock in the morning, and the masses were slowly dispersing. Most of the shops and cafes were closed, and many of the stranded passengers had surrendered their struggle in order to snatch slumber on available seats or portions of the floor where they could stretch out in comfort. I wandered around feeling more human with my belongings intact. I realised that there was nothing more I could do and gave up my own struggle, holding on to the belief that all would be resolved.

I was hungry and thirsty, and I needed to find an open store. Luckily, I had a few dollars in my little plastic bag and found a booth still selling coffee and a few stale sandwiches. I bought a stewed coffee and dry cheese roll, but I couldn't find anywhere to sit down, every seat and space was taken. I meandered into a large open area and sank down with my back against the wall, attacking the roll voraciously and washing it down with the hot liquid. The empty, silent space carpeted in a deep purple and red pattern was a no-man's land of bland nothingness, a void where life suddenly stopped for the night, and I began to feel uncomfortable in the dim light. There was no one around, and I could be attacked, left for dead, and no one would be the wiser! I got up wearily and trundled to an inhabited place. There were no spaces to bed down and my feet ached, so I decided that I would take my chances in the void, where I could at least stretch out! On returning, the lounge had become a bedroom for two other people who were now sleeping on opposite sides of the space. One was completely engulfed in his raincoat, which was folded over him like a tent, and the other lay stretched out next to his case, whispering quietly into his mobile.

Stillness hung like ancient tapestries in a desolate library at night. I felt safer with two other bodies in the purple dormitory and so slumped down, propping my rucksack on its side to use as a pillow, but it was lumpy and hard. I missed my poncho and began to feel chilly as the heat of the day died and the cold air conditioning pumped out clinical air freshener, which fought with the odour of stale bodies and overheated food. My eyelids were heavy and my eyes stung. A fatigue headache pulsed at the back of my head; after the fight and struggle, there was nothing left inside. I was drained, and a trickle of self pity began to dribble through my thoughts. I bit back the tears. What the hell was I doing stuck in limbo somewhere in Miami, decked out on the floor like a tramp? What would my children think? I had craved adventure. I had wanted to test myself, but all I wanted at that moment was to be safely tucked up in my bed back in my lovely cottage surrounded by my beautiful garden.

The sound of the air conditioning nagged into infinity reverberating on and on in the house of horror sleeping chamber as it transmuted into a macabre highway of spaceship machines driven by Halloween transport ghouls. Just as I was beginning to close my eyes, the first nightmare creature cycled past wearing massive khaki shorts and top, her black, round face shining in the half light, illumined by sweat as she transported miles of trolleys all bound together like a steel barricade. I had never seen such a weird apparition; it was almost funny, but I was too exhausted to laugh.

The second peculiar spectre appeared from nowhere with spaceship-like flashing lights twirling above a small motorised vehicle that sported protruding brushes, mops, and all manner of cleaning gadgets. The small goblinlike man-creature driving the contraption seemed stapled to it in a robotic way, moving mechanically as the device whirred, clanged, and clacked into action, cleaning the carpet and surrounding surfaces. The third and final spectre appeared on the purple heath a few moments later, hubbling and bubbling on an electric cleaning machine. He did not go up and down the space in regulation lines but rather wove spiral pathways, leaning over to the side as he turned sharp corners.

Just when I thought the macabre highway was clear, three policemen, all armed, strolled past me as though as I were invisible and entered a cleaning closet. It seemed a bizarre thing to do but was obviously a regular deviation from their nightly duty. I was near enough to the closet to hear the rustling of paper followed by male guffaws, gasps, and rasps of a sexual nature. They spent some time in the cubbyhole engrossed in their boys' meeting before walking off in different directions, looking officious. The macabre highway entertained me, and I was too wide-awake then to try to sleep, so I decided to quit my quiet spot and go back to see if there was a spare seat anywhere in the people place.

In the main passenger area, there were two seats free by an old lady who was sleeping with her head resting on her chest. Just as I was about to sit down, I spied the young man who had caused me much anxiety at the passport control check-in, and I felt slightly guilty at secretly venting my anger toward him, so I motioned with my hand that there was a spare seat beside me. He accepted my gesture, and we both sat down together, not realizing that the seats were faulty. We both fell backward comically, waking the poor old lady with a fright! Spontaneously, our laughter ripped across the sleeping bodies, waking most from their snatched slumber. It was wonderful to laugh with the stranger, and we struck up conversation instantaneously. He told me that his father was Italian, his mother Austrian, and he was living in Switzerland, which had caused some confusion at the passport control. I began to understand how wartime brought people together. It was refreshing to feel human again, sharing thoughts and ideas with someone. We ventured outside for a moment, walking like old friends, but the night was too hot and I was immediately attacked by mosquitoes.

Back inside, we bought coffee and related some of our lives to each other. Time raced by, and it was nearly six in the morning when we decided to wash and freshen up. Luckily there was no one in the lavatories, and I desperately needed to wash my feet. I was wearing new open-toed sandals, already cheesy and pungent from travelling. I was sticky with stale sweat and needed to change my underwear and brush my teeth, which I did in the privacy of the quiet cubicle. When I returned, Maris was waiting for me, and we briefly, naturally, exchanged a kiss before moving on. It was sweet and delicately sad; a frozen moment in time of pure friendship, never to be repeated, never to be forgotten.

There was no time to be sentimental, as the journey was under way. There were more control points to go through and check in my rucksack. More waiting, more time to think. The trip had put me through a rollercoaster of emotions, and yet, in the beginning of a new day, things were looking better. During the night at a bleak point, I had wanted to go home, but now I felt optimistic. A tiny child looked up at me from her mother's arms as we waited in the passport control queue. She wore a pink bonnet and smiled a toothless grin. Her deep blue eyes coyly lowered as I blew her a kiss. I wanted to hug her; she reminded me of my youngest daughter when she was a baby, and I remembered a strange incident, one of many in my life, where miracles do occasionally happen . . .

It was Monday morning and, with a new baby and three other children to get ready for school, life was chaotic! My eldest daughter, twelve years old, needed ingredients for her cookery lesson and was cross because there was nothing in the pantry, so I gave her the extra change I had in my purse to buy what she needed. My second daughter, nine years old, couldn't find her swimming things, which we had to retrieve from the hamper, and my three-year-old son was in tears because his favourite yellow car had been trampled underfoot by his sister! The new baby had made a horrible mess in the bath, and I had sprayed deodorant on my hair and hairspray under my armpits! I was in turmoil!

Holding baby in one arm, I opened my purse and spread the remaining change on the table to count out the lunch money for my two daughters, who waited impatiently by my side. There was just enough to cover the two lunches, which left me with nothing, not even enough to buy a cup of coffee! I wasn't unduly worried as, it being Monday, I could collect the family allow-ance; the problem was that the hard snowfall was turning to slush, which would make it difficult to push the pram into town, and I wasn't well, suffering with mastitis. I also had to walk to take my son to nursery school.

With a rising temperature, I slogged my way through the slush, delivering my son to his nursery school, and trudged into town. The early-morning delivery vans sprayed the pram with sludgy deposits, and my face was splattered with brown splodges. I wanted to cry. I was depressed, hungry, and in pain. None of the shops were open except Mothercare, and I ventured inside into the warmth, feeling better under the bright lights and cheery atmosphere. Large signs everywhere hailed "the Sale," and I meandered in and out of the large racks of tiny clothes, imagining my little one in a whole array of dresses. Hidden in a corner was a beautiful little coat of soft pink wool with a cerise fur hood. I fell in love with it immediately and took it off the rack. It had been vastly reduced from twelve pounds to five pounds fifty. I wanted so much to buy it for her, but I had no money.

A cold wind blew in from the street, gently ruffling the pink fur as I placed the coat carefully back on the rack. I thought someone was standing behind me and turned to look, but no one was there. I felt a presence, as though someone was sharing my thoughts. An electric tingle rippled through my chest, and I shivered. I looked at my watch. It was time to go to the post office and collect some money. I had food to buy and meals to prepare.

Just as I entered the old building, a lady came up to me and handed me a one-pound coin. She said she had seen it drop out of my pocket. I smiled and denied having the money, but she insisted I take it. I walked on a little further and watched a pound coin bounce off the top of my shoe. I couldn't believe it! There was no one around, so I put it in my pocket, totally bewildered. I sneezed, and, as I reached for a tissue from my other pocket, another pound coin dropped out! I laughed. It was a joke. I looked around expecting someone to ask for the money back. I joined the queue and a lady in front bent down and handed me a pound coin, saying I must have dropped it. I opened my mouth to deny it but just smiled instead. I had four pounds! I wasn't surprised when, just before it was my turn at the counter, a fifth coin landed from somewhere by the pram wheel. I had five pounds in a matter of a few minutes!

After collecting the family allowance, I opened my purse to put away the money. What I saw shocked me. The lady at the counter asked me if I was alright, and I smiled and walked away. Some small change lay at the bottom of my purse. It was fifty pence! From somewhere I had the exact amount of money to buy the little pink coat. In a state of elation and shock, I hurried to Mothercare and bought it. Whoever heard my plea granted my wish, whoever stood behind me in that time of need gave me what I desired, but more than that, gave me hope to believe in something beyond my routine existence.

Standing in the queue at the airport, a million miles away from that moment, I realised that wonderful things can happen at unexpected times. It's a matter of believing in oneself and trusting to the Universe that "all will be well, and all shall be well, as all is well."

The queue moved forward and the baby waved. I had a momentary pang of uncertainty, and I took a deep breath. Everything was going to be fine!

4

Cancun Connection

When I checked in at the main desk, I was composed. My flight to Cancun was scheduled to leave at ten-thirty that morning. Sighing with relief, I walked confidently down to the lounge and, while scanning the area, I saw a girl waiting with a rucksack. I thought she might be on the same trip, so I approached her. She was well built, wore glasses, and had a masculine face. I wasn't surprised when she introduced herself with a deep German accent. "Heldegarde; pleased to meet you."

Heldegarde was to travel with another group that would accompany us for a small part of the journey, and though I welcomed her purposeful nature, I was secretly glad she was not one of my party. The short hour's plane journey to Cancun was straightforward, and I was thankful to her for taking charge immediately when we landed. I was exhausted in the sweltering heat, and as she was familiar with the taxi system, so we were quickly sorted out after waiting in the long queue to change money in the crowded lobby.

Driving through the town in the packed minibus, I was shocked to see the extent of structural damage that the last hurricane had caused, reducing streets to rubble. But among the debris, unusual and beautiful sculptures had been erected, built in defiance of the next blow from Nature. June through November is the season for hurricanes, and I had been warned that it was a dangerous time to travel through Central America, but I was too excited to be fearful. My adventure was just beginning and, like a new mother who has forgotten the pain and trauma of labour and rejoices in the triumph of birth, I let the stress slip away and began to enjoy the ride.

I was disappointed with the hotel, which, true to the company's policy, was a low-budget guesthouse situated next to a restaurant and dry cleaners on the side of a main street. Inside, it was basic, cool, and colourful. After a few minutes, our young guide, Terrino, appeared. He was Chinese/African from New Zealand and beamed a wide welcoming grin. Suddenly the room began to swim, and I nearly lost my balance. Terrino acted quickly, and I was taken to a single room at the back of the hotel, where I fell exhausted onto the bed and slept until late afternoon. The room was adequate, and when I woke, I was hungry. Eagerly, I showered and changed my clothes, which I washed in the shower and hung to dry in the bathroom. I had so little clothes that it was necessary to wash things daily. Outside my room was a sunken tub cut in concrete under a washed-out tarpaulin in which sat four Mexican men and their families. They stared and stopped chattering as I went past on my way to the main lobby. There I found Heldegarde checking out information on the local amenities. I offered to take her to dine next door for looking after me in the airport and she readily accepted. The food was not brilliant, but she enjoyed it and I ate till I was full. Afterwards she suggested we explore the area, but I just wanted to relax and wait for my fellow travellers. I was curious to know what they would be like, so I sat in the small lobby by a vividly painted mural of sun, sea, and flowers, glad to be free of Hildegarde. People began converging on the meeting area, and when little Terrino appeared, four others took the sofa and spare seats—beautiful Maria, just seventeen, with classic Italian features and long, dark hair. Gunte, fresh from the German army, just twenty-four years old, was polite and shy. Gordon and Ella, from South Africa, were in their late fifties and "just friends," they explained.

We all introduced ourselves and I made polite conversation, looking at one another, making assumptions, accepting our fate together. Two more people were expected, but they had been detained by the terrorist plot and would join us in the morning. Two other women had opted out at the last minute because of the terrorist threat. I was a little disappointed that there wasn't anyone I could immediately relate to, but I was glad to make friends with the South Africans as we walked down the gaudy, noisy main street to our first meal together. I was still feeling a little groggy, and the bright lights of the shops decked with dazzling Mexican trinkets, hats, ponchos, and variety of traveller traps made me dizzy. I was glad to sit down at the wooden trestle table laid out down a side street of restaurants.

The atmosphere among us was light and jolly, with Gordon demonstrating his generous nature at the onset by ordering drinks for everyone. A little intoxicated, he danced the Mexican Hat dance, bouncing in the street, encouraged by the laughing musicians. The evening was a wonderful introduction to Cancun, with exotic food, catchy Mexican folk songs, and friendly chatter among the group, but I wished I had someone special to share the moment. The wine flowed, and I sank into a pleasant travel weariness. Back at the hotel, it was buzzing with the new group led by a confident young man from New Zealand named Vincent. I crept past Heldegarde, who was bossing a female in her group, and I was glad to close my eyes on the day's events, excited to begin the real adventure tomorrow.

I awoke the next morning feeling refreshed and happy, not overwhelmed by worries about making connections, and made my way to the breakfast area. I opted for the cooked meal and didn't mind paying extra for it, as I had a long day ahead. The Mexican breakfast was good, with the usual egg, bacon, sausage, but I didn't like the brown splodge, which was a specialty made from beans. Wearing my glasses to make some notes, the cracks in the crockery suddenly screamed at me along with the dirt and grime engraved in the plastic tablecloth alongside the grease-smeared coffee cup. I wondered momentarily why I had left all the luxuries of home behind, but on taking off my glasses, the world returned to its fuzzy calm, and I ate everything except the beans!

All bags packed, our little group met in the lobby to greet the last two members, a mismatched couple, newlyweds on their second marriages clinging to a relationship like the last autumn leaves bereft on a branch in a winter storm. Ava, sixty years of age, guarded this information uncomfortably, but Henry was open about nearly approaching fifty. Ava, with false tan and hair dyed jet black, was dressed in a low-cut floral sundress, revealing an aged flat chest, and wore ornate, open-toe sandals. She looked more prepared for a shopping spree in Oxford Street than a trek across the highlands of the Yucatan Province to explore one of the greatest temple sites in Central America, Chichen Itza. Both seemed in poor humour after their delayed flights and earned themselves the title of "the Complainers" from the rest of the group.

As Terrino led us across town to the bus station in the blazing early morning sun, the Complainers trundled suitcases in tow while the rest of us carried our regulation rucksacks and bags. We boarded an air-conditioned bus, our only luxury mode of travel on the trip, to take us to our first amazing step back in time, Chichen Itza. I took a window seat, and a little Mexican boy sat next to me, crying and stamping his feet in a very convincing temper tantrum, while his parents sat in the seat opposite with his baby sister. I tried to talk to the boy in my fragmented Spanish, but he continued to howl. I wrestled with the footrest, trying to get it to lie flat, but gave up despairingly. The little boy, obviously amused by my lack of mechanical knowledge, said in perfect English, "You do it like this!" Flabbergasted by his beautiful English, I smiled, and he stopped crying.

The bus was comfortable and was running a video film on penguins rearing their young on the ice, which was totally bizarre with the surroundings of suntanned Mexican families, browned tourists, and the inestimable heat outside. When we had cleared the city, miles upon miles of scrub-jungle, never-ending except for the damaged fallen trees crushed by the hurricane, was our only vista, with the occasional dead monkey lying spread-eagle against the dry, parched earth outlining the thick, harsh brush. On a major road I expected to see traffic, but on

25

the whole of the journey there was only one red van, which had been stopped to be searched by soldiers. This was considered a major road but was heavily potholed, ploughed like an English furrowed field in autumn, with unexpected soft, deep, muddy puddles that caused the driver to fight with the steering wheel to avoid swerving into the thick scrub-jungle. Our little driver was especially adroit at dealing with all the hazards, particularly considering that his feet hardly touched the floor and his tiny arms barely spanned the width of the wheel, but he seemed happy sucking a lollipop while listening to the local radio, heedless of the noise of the passengers or the Spanish-language documentary on how male penguins cared for their young. The soft, soporific bouncing of the bus lulled me into sporadic bouts of sleep, but I was too excited to indulge myself. Chichen Itza beckoned with a strange yearning.

I longed to witness what I had seen in books and photographs of the Temple of the Warriors, and the amazing and most famous of all pyramids, El Castillo, where at the sunset of the spring and autumn equinoxes the serpent rises from the bottom to the top of the pyramid, undulating in a magical spiral, dancing up the ladder of life. For a while, the bus was a safe, clean capsule where I could lie back and survey the dense jungle in comfort, not thinking about what lay ahead or my phobias about insects, snakes, spiders, and filthy accommodation. I was content to be a spectator, admiring the scrub from afar, happy in the penguin world of rearing babies on the ice, locked away from the heat outside, not realizing that my wish to challenge myself would soon be fully granted!

5

Chichen Itza

Chichen Itza, situated in the north of the Yucatan Peninsula, was one of the most powerful places for the Maya, taking its name from the opening of the two wells found in the area. The wells, or *cenotes*, were not only the life force of the community but were special open-air spaces where the chosen ones were slain in sacrifice to the gods.

Alighting from the bus, my stomach churned with excitement entering the lowland rain forest. Thick, lush overgrowth and scrub enclosed our party inside a peacock-green canopy. A massive overturned carved stone monument, breathtakingly crafted in an ancient time, loomed in a clearing. Abruptly I was face-to-face with it, staring into the eyes of the ritualistic dragonhead, left forlorn in its unkempt courtyard, while fragments of majesty lay in rubble around the fallen statues and the jungle crept inexorably into the cracks and crevices of the past.

We were led into a massive main arena where the parkland met the harsh jungle brush. Just a few steps in, the past became the present as El Castillo, the great Pyramid of Kukulkan, the snake god, loomed before us in all of its magnificence and primeval mystery.

As we waited for our guide, I touched the ancient bricks and wondered what it would have been like to be a citizen looking up at the plumed serpent magically ascending the great steps. Only a few days before, I had been standing in my little cottage garden, unable to imagine the power of that moment. Now, here, the calls of exotic birds, insects, and monkeys echoed through the dense rain forest, staking the present to the past. The high hills around us were not what they seemed, not just jungle, but more pyramids yet to be unearthed! We were surrounded by a thick mass of dense green, enclosed by layer upon layer of rain forest flora. It was fantastic to think that such a powerful city had been built in the ragged wilderness. The energy of those people was palpable in the air; I could smell it, breathe it. The vibration of the living stays hidden in the fabric of the space, it never dies, and the Mayan community was still there, like a distant memory hanging over the trees; loves and lives lost and found continued in the circle of forever.

Away to the left was the amazing ball court where major games were held and the losers slaughtered. Some of the skulls were used later as balls in a basketball-like game. The whole area heaved with warning of death as a curse, as a sacrifice, as a reminder that life is brief. Skulls engraved in the carved Wall of Death seemed to smile defiantly, eerily harking back to the space in time they once occupied as human beings. The skulls whispered through the bricks, daring to breathe their names again. The breeze took their sighs along the broken path where all is lost in the scattered debris of today.

Our soft-spoken Mexican guide was adamant that the sacrificial slaughter was not how it is portrayed in films; not the daily ritual slaying of children or young virgin girls. It was not the common occurrence to throw the sacrificed body down the pyramid steps to a bloodthirsty crowd below. I recalled the picture books I had seen of the bodies hurled down the flight of steps at the crack of dawn. The steep stairway loomed upward, and I imagined the ritualistic procession lead by the High Priests in their white and gold tunics, followed by servants holding high banners of multicoloured bird feathers that fanned the dawn air. The rising sun hit the first bricks at the bottom of the temple, luring the hidden snake out of its den, tempting it to rise to the top as the procession of the King and Queen in all their glittering splendour, and their children with the courtiers, ceremoniously climbed the sheer slope to heaven.

Our guide didn't deny that there probably were times when sacrificial slaughter was performed at the top of the temple, but it was more prevalent at the great *cenote* that we were about to visit. We left the parkland grass and the imposing temple to tramp through the forest, stepping inside the awning of lush green arches, it was darker here, brooding with past secrets. Our party, following the guide, was wrapped in quiet homage as we neared a clearing where the vast, stagnant, pea-green water gaped from a massive well. The *cenote* was much larger than I had imagined, and we beat a path through the dense scrub to stand on the rim, cautiously peering down as our guide explained that it was mostly thirteen-year-old boys who were sacrificed, and only on specific holy days. The child would be chosen at birth and born into the knowledge that he was a special child of the god Chac Mool, the rain god, and would be sacrificed in his honour. Throughout the child's thirteen years of life he would be allowed special privileges, and on the day of his death, he would be given a drug made of herbs so that he would not feel any fear or pain as the great sacrificial sword swiftly cut his throat. His body then would be thrown into the great *cenote*.

I stared hard into the green soup below, imagining the innumerable skeletons at the bottom. Offerings and ritual sacrifice were made to Chac Mool to ensure continued rich harvests. Suddenly, a boom of thunder cracked the day, piercing the gloomy sky with electric-pink lightning streaking above the dense jungle. "Chac Mool has spoken!" laughed our guide, and we all ran for shelter in the little gift shop set inconsistently against the brush. The tropical rainstorm beat thunderously against the small building and only abated slightly as we made our way back to the main site. A young boy stood in the clearing, grinning widely as he held out multicoloured plastic capes, which he was selling at inflated prices. I bought a bright yellow one and was glad of the little protection it offered.

The Mayans' vast knowledge of science, architecture, and astrology fused to create a fascinating place in the middle of the jungle. The question of how they built such amazing pyramids, where each brick fits perfectly in place, without the aid of modern, high-tech machines is a mystery. Where did they obtain the raw materials to build the structures; certainly they were not indigenous? How did they transport them? Our guide intimated that other beings, not of this world, had a hand in the process. Why did the civilization drop out of existence? Our guide told us that every few hundred years or so, the Mayans moved to a different location. The reason is not fully known, except that it was thought that the gods demanded it!

Looking at the faces of the bedraggled trinket-sellers sheltering in the forest, I could imagine the impact and force that beings from another sphere might have upon the natives. I had travelled to ancient sites all over the world, and the same stamp of celestial influence was here in the jungle as it was everywhere else. It has been suggested that the pyramids were towers built to communicate with extraterrestrial beings. The sense of something greater than humanity was unmistakably there, lurking, concealing secrets planted by beings with higher knowledge. As the warm rain splashed my eyelashes, the slight shock sent me to remembering when I stood next to an alien being, briefly, for a few seconds . . .

I was staying at my then-boyfriend's house. It was his birthday, and I had gone upstairs in his bedroom to collect his present. A fibre-optic light flashed gold, red, blue, silver from the corner, where I stooped to pick up the gift. As I turned round, the light flashing to gold, I froze. Standing next to me was a creature much taller than I, with gold, translucent skin. Inside his body I could see a mechanical structure that was gurgling, and bubbling. I felt repulsed. I had the impression for a fraction of a second that its face was like a hairless yeti. There were dark orbs where his eyes might have been, and his face, translucent like plastic gold, was sombre. It was neither good nor bad. I was traumatised by the encounter and fainted backward onto the bed.

That was all I could recall of the creature, and I hastily let the memory fade as I followed the others through the ball court. I was too tired to psychically tune into the past, although, fleetingly, I saw pictures that I thought were fancy. The previous day's travelling and stress was beginning to take its toll, so I was relieved when we made our way to the restaurant. It was late afternoon, and the small complex was flooded with wet tourists queuing for refreshment. A hot cup of coffee warmed my hands soothing me. I stood looking up into the triangular-shaped roof while the rain pounded, comforted for a while, knowing a fragment of infinity, an instant when I knew I could hold that second forever and relive it at will. It was a flash of understanding, of knowing who I was momentarily in a totally strange place. In that split second of comfort, I briefly knew happiness!

As I placed the plastic cup into the bin, the echo of multi-ethnic voices thronged through the darkening canopy as the day was drawing on. I was soaked to the skin and began to feel cold as we waited for a local bus to take us to Merida. I shivered and feared catching a chill, especially as I suffered from bouts of bronchitis, so I decided to change into a dry T-shirt. I scuffled through my backpack and found the nearest one. Deftly I changed my top underneath my plastic poncho, much to the amazement of the people around me. Years of dancing and doing instant changes had taught me quick tricks. I felt much happier in dry clothing. Such basic comfort made all the difference.

After a long, tiring wait, the old tin bus clanged its way toward us, and I found a seat near the back. Unfortunately the roof window was jammed open, but one of the men fought with the hinges and managed to close it. As we set off, a wave of fatigue overwhelmed me. My sodden feet ached. I inched off my sandals but was shocked to see that my feet were dark blue, stained from my shoes! As the rain beat down on our metal tank bludgeoning through the torrent, bouncing in and out of potholes, getting stuck in the thick mud, I felt like I was locked inside a biscuit tin that was being pelted with glass marbles.

The smell of wet wool and leather permeated the bus, making it feel strangely homely, especially as spirits were high after visiting Chichen Itza, and Merida just a few hours away. The idea of a new hotel, with food, a comfortable bed, and a shower was tantalizing. I did not know if I had to share or with whom, I just wanted to fold away all the discomfort and sleep. My eyelids grew heavy and, for a short while, I escaped the metal bar digging across my back on the hard seat and fell into a quiet slumber. After locking out the world for a while, I woke and hoped I hadn't snored or slept with my mouth open. The light had dwindled to the grey haze before twilight, and the bus was contentedly silent.

I reflected on the day's events. The storm and the flash of lightning just as Choc Mool's name was spoken hinted at the power and knowledge lost in the past. Lightning, such a supreme, natural element, is sent from the gods, sometimes in unusual places, to enlighten a spirit and awaken knowledge locked in the brain. Laurens van der Post, the famous South African writer and philosopher, recalled a time when he was a young boy walking across a vast expanse of grass in South Africa. It was a beautiful day, without a trace of a storm, when he was hit by a flash of lightning from nowhere that no one else saw. He believed that it was a divine happening and something that helped to open a channel of spiritual understanding. When I was seven years old, I had a similar experience. I was sitting at a small, circular table with five other children completing a math task with wooden bricks of all different shapes and sizes. We had to make a set pattern with the blocks, and our table was the first to finish. We sat up straight, delighted with our achievement, knowing that we would be the first to be let out for lunch. I looked up into the high windows of the old building, out into the grey, stark sky, when a terrific crack like a horsewhip, crashed across the table, and a blue streak of lightning lashed diagonally around my head. Thunder seared my ears as I threw myself across the table holding my head, scattering all the bricks over the dusty floor. I heard the teacher shout a warning from afar as the children jeered.

"The lightning, the thunder!" I shrieked. "Did you hear it?"

But no one had. Only silence reigned in the classroom as a naughty, rebellious, little girl disrupted the whole class by throwing herself over the table, destroying her friends' work, making them all stay behind to clear up the mess and making them the last to go to lunch! No one believed me. No one saw the lightning or heard the thunder. No one spoke to me. I was ostracised for my rebellious behaviour, but inside my head, a door had opened.

In the electric, tropical glow of twilight, our tin transport pulled up in the bus station in Merida. The tropical afternoon rain had refreshed the grimy streets and overflowed the gutters, gurgling as we ran a race with the small rivers down the road, wet feet splashing, squelching in the rush to get to the hotel. My bad leg ached, but I pushed myself to keep up with the others, my rucksack bouncing painfully on my back as I limped to an new adventure.

6

Merida: Gateway to the Mayan Ruins of Uxmal

The now is winter, and I am thankfully still living in my lovely quaint cottage, and I have not been imprisoned for tax evasion. The now of yesterday is then, and the moment mingles with future plans. I have learnt that all is; nothing else. I have not forgotten to forget what I should remember, though it would be easy to do so amid the clatter and clamour of routine existence. The diurnal round ticks off the minutes of each day, acknowledging the passing of weeks, which somehow dwindle into the stale melancholy of years long gone. I sit sipping hot coffee in my power kitchen, newly designed with sparkling red-granite counter tops and a black ceramic sink. So modern, so new, so me! I ponder how time is such a strange commodity. It is not what we have devised it to be. We have the ability to bend it, shake it into a format to suit the moment, but it takes much concentration and energy, an ability outside the norm. I have used this facility only a few times in my life, for my children.

The snow falls gently outside the kitchen window, softly decorating my ancient cherry tree in a white lace shawl. The twinkling mirrors I planted in the branches glisten with pre-Christmas tidings, while the bleak, monochromatic sky predicts more storms. I must prepare for school and scrape the snow from my car, as I must plan for the day and scrape emotion from the pit of my stomach, where it grazes the lining of my gut as it surges up into my throat. The bitter taste of fate bites. She died instantaneously, they said; she didn't feel any pain as the truck ploughed into her head-on. She was riding her bicycle listening to her music– so many times I had warned pupils of the danger of not being able to hear the traffic! She was a wonderful student, a star in Drama and now there is emptiness where there was once laughter. You bright, blood-red jewel shining in the dark drama studio, feeling your way through new characters. I watched you grow and experiment with your brief life. It doesn't seem fair, but I know that everything has a purpose, and wherever you are now, you are. I had not been prepared for this kind of attachment when I had returned to teaching; it caught me out one innocent morning when her death was whispered in a corner and my anguished cries hit the cold, white walls, clearing the staff room.

The now is winter. The now is old—cold, but I will not drive into the blizzard, I will steer into the then of heat, the then of adventure, the then of complete acceptance in an exotic land blitzed with colour. I feel the hot, humid heat in the creases of my body, sweat trickling down my back, drenched from head to toe in the warm, tropical torrent as I scurry across the waterlogged streets of Merida.

Evening is a sigh, a quiet pause before the rush of nightfall. Darting across the uneven streets to the Hotel Barracuda, my backpack stuffed underneath my plastic cape, was like running the one-mile dash to victory. "Just a few more paces!" I kept promising myself. I had to keep up with the others, afraid I might be abandoned and lost in the great city. I pushed my weary body into action. Eventually we reached the hotel, where we stood in the amazing lobby, dripping wet and laughing with a sense of achievement. After sleeping on the bus, I was energised and ready to adapt to the hot-humid evening. The hotel must have been quite a place years ago. It was odd to come in from the street into a museum filled with exotic artefacts, paintings, and furniture. It lacked the hand of the woman who had lovingly created it with artistic flair. I sensed her presence and knew that she had long departed, leaving her partner to juggle the business alone; unfortunately he had not kept up the magnificence she had designed, nor the basic cleanliness.

Hotel Barracuda was my first experience of the Latin American house built around an open courtyard with a view of the sky, exposed to all weather, forest scrub thriving in the midst of everyday living. To the right of the open jungle was a small, concrete building with a rough, corrugated roof. The kitchen! Bits of concrete rubble lay on the floor around the base. No one had bothered to clean it up or tidy the remnants of the building materials left scattered on the lovely tiled floor. The owner, George, was English, from Newcastle, and stood behind the bar dealing out keys with a pleasant, welcoming smile. I was to share with Maria, and we were led through a maze of walkways that were once glamorous, tastefully adorned with colourful, handcrafted pots placed strategically in corners to reflect the light. Tiny nightlights and candles spread out near hanging hammocks, but in the humid night, the smell of rotting plaster and decaying paint was all that remained of the artistic flair that had carefully pieced it all together. Little lights and lanterns twinkled amidst the forest scrub splashed with raindrops from the great downpour, sparkling like white diamonds in a grotto.

We were down a small corridor to our room. It was peculiar, with the outside wall built entirely of mirrors. When the light was on, you could see in from outside, and when the light was off, you could see outside from inside. There were two single beds and a cupboard and as I laid my rucksack on the floor, I peered under the bed and was almost sick. Underneath was a thick carpet of dust and grimy debris. The room had not been cleaned properly for years. One of my phobias was filth; my skin began to crawl and itch with imaginary creepies. I pushed the thought of insects and rats to the back of my mind and smiled at Maria, who was unpacking. I couldn't bear the thought of taking out my clean clothes and laying them on the bed. The cover was not clean, although the sheets beneath were. The bathroom had some semblance of cleanliness but stank of open sewers and rotting vegetables. The smell emanated from an open grate near the tiny sink. I was afraid to imagine what might be lurking below, watching me with beady eyes! The place was a hellhole! I showered hastily, trying not to breathe in the foul stench. My feet were dyed blue, and no amount of scrubbing shifted the colour. I fought to subdue my rising anxiety about the lack of cleanliness, reminding myself that it was a challenge, something I needed to do battle with and overcome!

Our small party had a meeting in the billiard room to decide on activities for the next day, but I couldn't afford any of the extra activities and made excuses about wanting to be free to explore the city. The Complainers complained bitterly about many aspects of the trip as the rest of us listened uncomfortably. It was arranged for us to have an evening meal together in a small café, but I had only a limited budget and chose one of the least expensive dishes, while Terrino, whose food was free, had the best of everything and made us all wait for our main course as he indulged himself in a huge starter. The food was adequate but not amazing; however, I enjoyed my single glass of red wine while the Complainers ordered a bottle of wine for themselves.

Terrino fancied himself as a salsa dancer and took some of us to a place where we could try out our moves. Sometimes a magical moment is born out of nowhere, without warning. The enchantment happens and then disappears, like Cinderella when the clock strikes twelve. I was dancing with our group when a man appeared from the crowd and swept me into a spin. We instantly knew each other's steps. The floor cleared and the crowd watched as we twisted, turned, and gyrated to the electric pulse. When the first dance finished, the crowd demanded more, so we performed in a bubble of light, two strangers lost in a language of timeless rhythm. But then, like Cinderella, it was time to go back to my dingy quarters. I only had time to learn his name, Rodrigo, and to say good-bye. It was a brief moment when the Dance is all and ever shall be.

Back at the hotel, I was dreading sleeping in the bed. An irrational nausea crept up my throat, and I wanted to cry. Maria was not bothered, and I had to conquer my silly fear, as I couldn't appear ridiculous in front of her. I inched my way down the bed and tried not to feel itchy and scratch my skin raw. I was afraid that creepy crawlies would invade my bed while I was sleeping, as once happened in India, when a huge nest of red ants made a meal out of me in the dead of night! The air was hot and there was no air-conditioning, but I pulled the sheet tight over my head. I couldn't sleep and was disturbed when I heard voices outside the room. Our light was off, so I could see outside in the dimly lit corridor. It was Terrino and a young girl hungrily exploring each other's bodies. I didn't want to be part of their sexual encounter and tried to sleep through it, feeling glad when they finally departed. For the rest of the night, I drifted in and out of sleep and was relieved when morning came.

Breakfast was a meagre affair, with sliced white bread, butter, and jam set out under the corrugated concrete sty. Diluted powdered orange juice was available with stewed tea or coffee. I barely ate or drank anything, as I intended to find somewhere in the city to eat. I watched as members from both parties left together to explore their various activities while I sat quietly by the edge of the indoor jungle feeling sorry for a pathetic little bird in a golden cage whose scant, yellow body with its skimpy red plumage and bare tail feather hung upside down. I guessed that he must have been a pet of the lady who had created the wonderful art gallery, as no one seemed to care about him now. Perhaps he was part of her lost world, only fed, watered, and covered over at night. I wanted to set him free.

By eleven o'clock, the hotel was quiet, with only an old woman cleaner and a handy man padding around, so I decided that it was time to make my first solo expedition into the center of Merida. I needed a special plug adapter to charge my phone and some other things. The light was bright as I passed through the main door into the street. The sun was already high and the heat intense. I took a photograph of the hotel and looked around to get my bearings. I knew that I would reach the main square if I walked in a straight line. I had always wanted to sit in Merida park and people watch, like Carlos Castaneda's character, Don Juan, a sorcerer who could see peoples' auras. Having studied

Casteneda's "Magical Passes" in Berlin and read all his work, I was keen to try my hand.

The white pavements and stark walls glared as the dazzling light bounced off my sunglasses, making my eyes water. The small streets were quiet, and only a few small shops were open. I ventured into one filled from top to bottom with native handcrafts. I bought some beautiful cushion covers in kitschy colours together with a pair of hand-woven shorts. Feeling happy with my spoils, I reached the square. The sun was scorching my back, so I sat down under some trees for shade. I began to feel uncomfortable as eyes focused on me from all directions. I gave up my intention to people watch and decided to go on an adapter search on the opposite side of the square. The masses had begun to gather, thronging in groups and family units outside the main shops. They all gawked as I hurried by. I remembered the feeling from my first trip to India where people stopped and stared blatantly. It was unnerving. I escaped into an electrical shop. Shakily, I asked for the plug in basic Spanish. The man understood me and gave me what he thought was best. It was very cheap and as I braced myself to face the crowds again, I began to wish I had not been so confident and self-assured about walking alone. It was foolhardy; a blonde-haired woman in a sea of ebony faces was bound to attract attention.

Bending my head toward the ground, I scurried back to the square. It was unbearably hot and my body was bathed in sweat. I wished I had worn a hat not only to hide from the sun but to conceal my embarrassment. Momentarily the square looked unfamiliar, but I was sure I had plotted out my route and knew exactly how to get back to the hotel. I was certain that it was the next side street. A wave of fear washed over me as doubt cloyed at my certainty, but I brushed it aside. The idea of being lost was terrifying! No one knew where I was, they wouldn't even know if I got lost! With rising panic, I paced down the side street searching for a familiar landmark, but I didn't recognise anything. It was baking hot, the sun scorched my shoulders, my head ached, and my eyes stung. I felt sick and empty in my stomach, remembering that I hadn't eaten or drunk very much that morning. I raced on a little further but knew it was pointless. It was not the right street.

I suddenly realised alarmingly that I couldn't remember the name of the hotel! Turning back down the street, I fought to remember it. My mind went blank. I must know the name! I knew it earlier. My body was burning, my brain boiling, I couldn't think straight! I stopped walking. People gaped. It had to be the next street, surely it was the next street? I felt dizzy. On reaching the square, I gazed at all four corners, the church, the shops, the market, the art shop—it was all jumbled. I didn't know which way to go! I was lost, alone, and frightened!

I leaned my back against a wall in the shade and tried to disintegrate into the bricks, not wanting anyone to see my panic. I couldn't swallow, my heart was pounding, and sweat trickled along my scalp and down my neck. I was confused. I tried to think of the name of the hotel, tried to see it psychically. Then I remembered that I had taken a photograph of it earlier. I rummaged in my bag for my camera and rewound the takes. There it was, the Hotel Barracuda! I sighed, relieved to at least have one lead. I searched the crowd for a friendly, approachable face and saw a man in a uniform. I nervously asked him where the hotel was, and he told me there were two named Barracuda. My heart sank. I asked directions for the nearest one to the square and he pointed down a street on the opposite side. Somehow I had become completely disorientated in the heat and panicked. I spotted shops and doorways I now recognised, and began to relax, feeling my fear fade away, promising myself never to be so stupid again. The shock of being lost had taught me never to wander too far away alone, the abject feeling of desperation and bleak fear was something I didn't ever want to experience again.

I spotted a small café and calmly entered the cool, clean restaurant. It was bracing to feel the cold air like the first sea breeze on a summer's day back home at the seaside. I ordered three drinks, one exotic juice, one alcoholic cocktail, and a cup of coffee. My release from my misadventure had made me extravagant. The waiter looked at me strangely. Then I ordered three separate dishes. Again he was perplexed but took my order. The drinks were wonderful and the food excellent. Feeling refreshed and in control, I walked confidently back to the hotel. On returning to the room of mirrors, I tried not to look too closely at the walls, but my gaze rested on a huge cobweb in the corner just above my bed with a gigantic spider suspended in the middle. I ran out of the room and grabbed hold of the old lady, who was still plodding along the corridors with her mop and broom. When she saw the spider, she understood and called the handyman, who came and climbed on the bed and brushed it away, but it scampered somewhere, and I was left wondering where it was hiding, which was almost worse than watching it watching me! I couldn't stand being in the room with it, so I made my way to the lobby and sat in a large, colonial-style red leather chair opposite the jungle mass. It was like having a ringside seat in a virtual-reality game.

Suddenly the sky darkened. There was a moment's pause before the sky cracked and torrential rain flooded. It was surreal sitting on the edge of a dense overgrowth in a comfortable armchair yet being part of the open storm. After the intense heat of the morning, the rain was cooling and cleansing, refreshing the whole building. The quiet moment was broken by a crowd of young men entering the hotel hovering over Maria, who had cut her head in the street on a protruding bar. She sat beside me and was swamped with attention. She was a little shaken but was fine. The young men were from the other group travelling with us and were keen to offer their support to her. The dark storm thickened, and sheets of lightning shot across the room, electrifying the bar with pink streaks. Within a few minutes the lobby was swamped with everyone returning from their activities. Large puddles formed around the forest scrub as the rain pelted down, forcing people to jump across to go to their rooms. The atmosphere was friendly as people shouted to one another above the voice of the storm.

Just as quickly as the storm struck, it calmed, leaving the fresh smell of wet earth hanging in the air. Afternoon diminished into the gentle lull of evening as we prepared to take to the streets to watch the dance festival. In a bright bar, people related

41

the day's events, but I kept mine a secret; I was too embarrassed to admit I got lost! The drinks flowed before we drifted out into the main square to watch the colourful folk dances of Merida. We sampled the local drink, cochinita pibil, and El Yucateco, a fiery elixir made from habanero peppers. The rhythm throbbed through the night as we continued our group perambulation from bar to bar until we returned en masse to the wacky museum quarters of Hotel Barracuda, saturated in the old colonial style with stuffed animal heads glaring in the gloom, their fixed glass eyes following everyone.

Maria and I made our excuses to the group, as we had an early start in the morning. I was pleased that it was our last night there because the thought of the large spider lying in wait somewhere in the room filled me with dread. Once in bed, I drew the sheet up over my head in the stifling heat and waited for sleep to engulf me, trying not to imagine it crawling onto my bed and creeping over my sleeping body. I cheered myself with the thought that I was not still wandering around Merida lost and alone. I was disappointed not to have indulged my long-held ambition of sitting in the main square in Merida people watching, but it was not to be. I had not practiced aura gazing for a while, not since the time in class when I was overwhelmed to see a teenage girl's bright, beautiful aura quite unexpectedly, as I was giving a long speech about Shakespeare. I stopped mid-sentence and stared in her direction. She had long, bright red hair that hung loosely over her shoulders and a pale, freckled complexion. Suddenly, three layers of light, mostly gold, encircled her head and shoulders. The class stared back at me, wondering what was wrong, and, as I sat down at my desk to pause, I willed the aura to disappear. My ability to see auras seemed to have dwindled after that.

I struggled to sleep, wondering if Terrino would appear again on one of his night adventures with the ladies, but fortunately, the only sound was the crickets droning on into the early hours before dawn which crept through the mirrored windows, streaking the dirty walls with a bright glow, luring me to get up with the thrill of travelling to the Mexican highlands to search out the lost city of Palenque.

7

Palenque:
My Stumble into the Past

Love is the only resonance, the purest vibration
in the universe which brings total harmony. . .
                              —*L.A. Eden*

After a meagre breakfast from the tin shack, both parties joined up for the bus to Palenque. The bus weaved through jungle and brushy scrubland trying to avoid large potholes and almost impassable mudflats, until the lush Chiapas jungle's exotic wildlife and tropical flora encompassed us. Just before the bus drew to a halt, we passed a lorry loaded with distressed pigs being driven to the slaughterhouse. They were piled high to the top of the lorry, some of them turned upside down with their feet kicking the air. I was shocked to see how mercilessly they were transported, but I had to remind myself that we were deep in the wilds of nowhere!

Palenque, one of the most famous and impressive achievements of the Maya, lies in the middle of the dense jungle. The ancient city houses over two hundred buildings, with temples, tombs, houses, and courtyards. The temples are extraordinary, set in a place of total serenity. I had never and will never stand in such a place. The Earth's vibration resonates pure tranquillity. The peace is beyond knowing. In a single breath, I could ingest a timeless energy and allow myself to feel the pulse of the Great Ones dancing to their songs in my mind. The atmosphere was electric. The pulse tingled around me. I knew that beings beyond our Earth had dwelt there. The cave painting of King Pakal inside his tomb shows him inside his sarcophagus, but if you turn the drawing on its side, he is definitely inside a space capsule!

The morning was fresh as we stood on the dewy grass shaded by the hills and massive temples. Looking up into the amazing architecture, the question of how the temples were built so meticulously without modern instruments was again posed by the guide. It was the same mystery as at Chichen Itza. We were led down the slippery sloping steps to King Pakal's tomb, where his mummified remains were found in 1952. His stone sarcophagus lay empty in the stillness of the tight enclosure. Further on, we came to small courtyards whose walls still displayed decorations and sculptures, though they had lost their vibrancy and colour. I imagined scenes from the past, hearing people talk as they went about their daily chores.

I was engaged on another vibration, high on a different frequency, open to connecting with the lost world, receptive to other beings, so it wasn't surprising that, when I paused by an ornately decorated frieze, a spirit came to me. He was Ella's deceased husband. This was not unusual or frightening. All my life I have been connected to the spirit world and am used to communicating with energies. He spoke gently, but it was not possible at that time to tell her. I didn't know her very well and felt I couldn't help. Always I am given a message to pass on so that the recipient knows the connection is real, and, as I pondered his words, we were led to the top of a temple, where there was only a thin broken ridge to tread our way around. I couldn't believe that we were perched on the very top of the temple and expected to ease our way around the dangerous ledge. We all cautiously manoeuvred one foot at a time as the brick crumbled and dropped below. In places, the brick had deteriorated completely, leaving a gaping hole with a view straight down. When I reached one of these, I froze. I had never been afraid of heights before, and the gap was only about six inches long, but I couldn't step across. My legs began to quiver and my body turned to stone. It seemed easier just to fall. I wanted to fall! Suddenly, hands held my waist from behind. Gordon whispered, "I've got you! You can do it!"

There was something in his voice that I instinctively trusted. My legs moved and my feet stepped across the void as more shale crumbled away. I managed to make it and climbed down the steep, open steps until I was safely back on the ground. I thanked Gordon profusely. He was a kind gentleman. Ella smiled supportively. I wanted to tell her about her husband but didn't have the courage.

Perhaps my connection with the power of the place and my communication with Harry, Ella's husband, and my panic attack at the top of the temple had drained the colour from me, making Gordon and Ella protective. They walked with me through the meandering steps down the forest. It was so beautiful. The heat of the day was just beginning to penetrate the jungle mass, and I was relieved to see in the distance a long, wooden building, open at the sides, with tables, chairs, and people sitting enjoying some refreshment. I was thirsty and looked forward to sitting down. The building was dark and welcoming from the intense heat. I was just about to step across the road to enter the building when Ella stopped me sharply with her arm. She prevented me from walking out onto a main road as a van shot around the corner. I stood on the verge, shocked.

"But where's the restaurant? The wooden building?"

Both Gordon and Ella looked puzzled.

"There isn't anything, only trees!" stated Ella.

I was sure there was a building, a dark wooden structure with a long, slightly lighter wooden floor. I saw it. I saw people. Ella took my arm gently as we walked across the tarmac road. I was stunned. They took me to a shady place under some trees to wait for our bus. Ella was receptive to my experience, and she admitted that she was also psychic. She understood that I had connected with the past and witnessed a scene from long ago. I had entered a vibration on a much deeper level than I had realized, and coming out of it was a shock. The wooden building stood quite clearly a few yards away, open-fronted with people relaxing inside! To see only brush and scrub jungle in its place was perplexing. As I sat waiting for the bus, I tried to come to terms with what I had seen. I could re-create it in my mind, it was not imagined.

At Palenque, we split from the other group for a while and took a minibus to the nearby Agua Azul and Misol-Ha waterfalls. The bus ride gave me chance to absorb my strange experience. The waterfalls area is an amazing beauty spot set high in the mountains. As we left the bus at the foot of the mountain track, we walked in single file, following Terrino through the lush tropical forest. Near the base of the waterfall, nature was interrupted by a fairground setting, with small market stalls selling all kinds of trinkets, food, batteries, fruit, and medicine. We stopped near what appeared to be a gypsy camp, with an open fire and ancient grate over the top.

"This is where we will eat lunch!" stated Terrino, who was always hungry.

Our small party accepted whatever he dictated. Having lived in India, I was wary of eating in such a place where hygiene was not strictly observed. I watched as the young Indian man chopped pieces of chicken on an old wooden board and handed them to his wife, who placed them on the grill over the open fire. She set out plates on a rickety old table and dished out mixed vegetables from a plastic container. The smell of the barbequed chicken by the waterfall was enticing, and I gave in to my hunger pangs, tucking into the meal along with the others. It was extremely cheap, and the young Indian couple were grateful for the tip we left them.

Everyone changed into their swimming things except me. I was not a swimmer and feared the water, but everyone was grateful to have someone stay behind and watch their things while they swam. In truth, I needed a little space to mull over my experience at Palenque. I had slipped into another dimension unexpectedly and needed to recover. I had definitely seen the long wooden building. I had taken it for granted that it was of our time. I had seen people sitting there, relaxing, talking, drinking while children played at their feet, and the jolt into reality by nearly being knocked down by a van shot me back into the present unexpectedly.

This breathtakingly blue lake perched high in the mountain forest gave the families wonderful freedom to have fun. My childhood had not been like that. Our Sundays consisted of Mass in the morning and Catechism class in the afternoon, followed by a Sunday tea ritual. It was during one such Sunday tea that I learnt for the first time I was different from the rest of my family.

I was four years old and my little brother, two and a half. We had to sit quietly at the tea table and eat everything on our plate. My brother, all sweetness and innocence above the table, smiled while taking hefty shots at my shins with his sturdy boots under the table. I occasionally got him back when he wasn't expecting it; then his smile would crack for a second before turning on the beam again. Neither of us could display any reaction in case we were caught and severely punished. Just as I was about to take a crack at his leg, something moving in the field distracted me. It was spring, and the bright, verdant grasses quivered in the meadow as the great hawthorn bushes, heavily laden with white blossoms, danced in the playful breeze. A stranger came riding past the brook dressed in Victorian riding clothes. She was a vision in black from head to toe, trailing a long, meshed veil that was stretched over her pale, luminescent face. Her long, sleek skirt, curtained across the horse's smooth, shiny flank, gleamed midnight blue in the sunlight. I gazed at her with curiosity. I had never seen anyone so beautiful and graceful. Her eyes stared back at me, boring into my head. She was so far away, yet her face was close to mine, sucking me into a deep treacherous void.

I was terrified and shot under the table, spilling food everywhere. My father growled and dragged me back to the table. My brother jeered under his smile. He always thought it funny when I was punished. I sat back, staring at the white table cloth, trying to understand what had happened. I glanced sideways to see if she was still there. She was galloping wildly toward the house. I saw her beautiful face drawing close to mine, feeling her black eyes squeezing me in a twisted grasp until I couldn't breathe, and again I crashed under the table shouting, "It's the lady, the lady on the horse!" My father lost his patience, as he couldn't see the lady or the horse.

"She's making up stories again!" said my mother as she searched the field with her eyes. No one else could see the lady or the horse!

I was severely punished and sent to bed. I couldn't understand why they couldn't see the woman, she was so real to me. My bottom stung from the hiding, but worst of all, I felt totally alone. I knew that I must never again say what I was really seeing. I was confused by the different realities, mine and theirs. Why couldn't they see what I saw? It was a conspiracy against me! I was not like them and had never fit into their world. I lived in two worlds, theirs and mine, and I had to find a way to live in both!

At Palenque, watching the joy of families swimming together in an idyllic paradise where the electric-blue water cascaded down the lush jungle mountainside and crashed into a basin below, made me adjust to the moment and soak in a unique scene. I felt privileged to be there and glad to be of some help to the others, allowing them to swim in peace, knowing that their belongings were safe. They were so grateful when they returned, and that gave me a good feeling, at least something was real in my forever-changing perception of reality.

8

Visitation in the Isthmus of Tehuantepec

W here am I now?
On a train travelling back to my past.

She implored over the phone, "Come and see him before it is too late!"

Will the past be erased in one embrace?

I was always a cuckoo in their nest. Why was I theirs?

I remember my birth with death clinging to my face like a wet rag. They were told I wouldn't last the night! How wrong they were!

It is three days before Christmas, so I go bearing gifts. The lost wanderer returns but not for long: long enough to say good-bye.

The rural landscape rushes passed unlocking memories of woodland walks and farmyard antics. I know these fields, these brooks and yet all I really know is this moment. I had yesterday, I may know tomorrow, but if I fall off the edge of reality now, then all I will know will be the present. My reason argues that I must accept them as they are now, not what they were or did. Forget blame, forget the sour taste of hurt.

Where am I now?

On the train going home. I have a peaceful heart. One embrace, embracing all in forgiveness, is all that was necessary. Father, mother known again.

Forgiveness is easy to say but hard to execute. The message from Harry, Ella's deceased husband in Palenque, was a private matter, and I hesitated to help, but after sharing my experience of stepping back into the past with Ella and Gordon, it was easier to broach the subject of his visitation. After the wonderful waterfall interlude, we boarded the small bus to our next evening's location deep in the heart of the jungle. I was able to speak to Ella on the bus and was relieved that the message made sense to her. It was a secret code which only she could understand, and it moved her deeply.

We arrived at our next location late in the afternoon and met up with the other group, who were busy relaxing in the swimming pool in the dense jungle. Tiny huts had been built amid the thicket of palms, bamboo, and luscious trees. Maria persuaded me to join them in the swimming pool, but I stayed for only a few moments, as the water was greasy with everyone's sun protection, plus flies and large insects were floating on the surface. After a full day's events, most of us were tired and hungry, but Terrino decided that we would get a better deal just down the road, where there was a large restaurant with live open-air entertainment. Ostensibly it seemed a good idea, but by the time we set out, it was pitch- black. We couldn't even see our hands in front of our faces! Gordon was fatherly, protective, and held my hand during the long walk. We were careful to follow the clear road that had been hewn through the dense jungle, but the night creatures kept us alert with their shrill shrieks and warbling warnings. The air was clean and clear, and I breathed deeply, like thirstily drinking cool, sweet water from a fresh stream. The night was a single black blanket, both sky and earth one mantle, except for the bright, starry beacons pulsing in the stillness. The trudge seemed endless.

Eventually when we arrived, the place was packed and waiters were scurrying around looking annoyed. We waited for a while amidst the din and clatter of plates until we were shown to a table. There we waited for over an hour for some bread! The Complainers complained bitterly, and Ava, Mrs. Complainer, kept falling asleep at the table, she was so weary and long past hunger, looking pitiful as the insects buzzed around her legs and arms. Gradually as the restaurant quieted, we were served our food, but by this time Ava, outraged, left, dragging her husband behind like a lost sheep. In the quiet, we moved to a table under a huge canvas, where the cabaret was about to begin. I was not impressed by the jugglers, two English girls in multicoloured Lycra tights who could barely catch a ball. One in particular kept dropping hers under the tables and had to scramble awkwardly underneath to retrieve it. Gordon, Maria, and I agreed it was time to make tracks. There were no taxis, so we prepared ourselves for the long walk, leaving the others, who by that time had consumed enough wine to make the entertainment palatable. Exhausted, we trekked in the blackness to the dimly lit campus.

Maria and I were to share again, but as she had an assignation with a boy from the other group, I went to our little jungle hut alone. Fearful of insects and snakes, having been bitten by a poisonous snake in the swamps in New Orleans, and my frightening experience with red ants in India made me very wary of high rafters, dark corners, and strange beds, so I shuffled down under the covers again in the heat of the night to hide from any interloper.

In the morning, we had breakfast with the other group in the large campus restaurant, helping ourselves to cereal, toast, and yogurt. Maria made her sad good-byes to the boys in the other group, as we were parting company that morning to travel our separate ways. On the tiny bus, Terrino explained that although we were going south, we were driving through the Chiapas mountain highlands and could expect to feel colder after the intense heat in Yucatan. Travelling through the highlands, which is a more traditional part of Mexico, we would encounter Indians who rarely came into contact with foreigners, and it was important to respect their customs and not annoy them by taking photographs without their permission. We were heading towards

51

the Isthmus of Tehuantepec and the Chiapas Mountains, where the villagers were mostly from two Indian groups, the Tzotzils and Tzeltals. Terrino further explained that the mode and style of dress of the Indians changed according to the indigenous groups of the area. The Tenejapans wore knee-length black tunics, and the Chamulans white wool tunics, whereas the Zinacantecos wore multicoloured outfits with ribbons on their hats, signifying the number of children they had. He said that we had to be very careful of one group of Indians who were overtly aggressive if they saw anyone pointing a camera at them.

It was exhilarating to ride through miles of untouched mountain jungle in our minibus, bouncing through chains of volcanic lakes and exotic forests. I had seen films of the area, but actually being there was thrilling! We were heading for the ancient state capital of San Cristobal de las Casas, which stands high in a mountain valley and is steeped in wonderful examples of sixteenth-century architecture, with amazing churches embossed with colourful decorative detail. For four and a half hours, we wound our way through the mountains, feeling the change in the atmosphere as the jungle merged into forest and the forests turned into lush meadowland. It was a relaxing journey, and Ella and I got to know each other better and disturbed the silence of the bus with fits of girlish giggles.

By the time we reached San Cristobal, it was early evening, and the city was buzzing with life. Bright light spilt onto the slippery wet cobbles from the open shops that oozed tantalizing smells of fruity spices and barbequed chicken. We scurried along the narrow streets until we reached an arched entrance. Inside was a large open courtyard with a single white wall enveloped in purple bougainvillea and long corridors of dark oak doors leading off both sides. Maria and I were shown to our small cell up a typically Spanish black wrought-iron staircase. Upstairs the quiet air of a harshly disciplined convent pervaded our small room with its stark walls and varnished wooden single beds.

The Complainers urged Terrino to find a good place to eat that night, and he obliged by taking us to an amazing restaurant. We entered through large, ornately carved double wooden doors into a medieval, magical paradise, where we sat on cushions at a low table to order Thai food. The colourful lanterns and unusual lights added a touch of the East to a very Mexican setting. The wine was good, and we all gelled as a group for the first time, laughing and joking, releasing tensions that had built up during the journey.

Back at the convent-style hotel, Maria shivered in the cold night air. We had become accustomed to hot, sticky nights and found the Chiapas chilly. It was fiesta time, and the night silence was broken intermittently by fireworks and flashes of gunshots ricocheting down the long, open corridors. It ceased in the early hours of the morning, to be resumed later that day.

We walked to breakfast through a typical Mexican square, where the men banded together smoking in corners, wearing white Stetson hats, ornate, hand-woven ponchos, high-heeled cowboy boots, and embroidered shirts in the traditional Mexican style. Other Chiapas Indians wore tunics and strutted across the square like peacocks underneath the imposing red and yellow church, where feathery white lacework decorated the statues of the Madonna. It was a truly different world from the Yucatan Peninsula, with the locals more suspicious of the visitors, except for the hippie crowd, who tended to laze around on the steps, merging with some of the Indians in a haze of smoke.

The restaurant was immaculate and beautifully designed, with huge, handcrafted blue pots on display. The high walls were decorated in different hues of azure, and an occasional splash of red ochre highlighted the cool, tranquil seascape. Unfortunately, the Complainers were complaining about each other, arguing in front of everyone, putting a damper on the morning, and the group as a whole was embarrassed by their inability to blend peacefully into the party. As usual, Ava dressed as though she were going out to tea, adorned lavishly with long, dangly earrings and matching accessories instead of dressed for a mountain adventure.

After demolishing the traditional Mexican breakfast (minus the brown bean mess), I was ready to face the morning's travel in the local guide's van. We headed for the mountain villages.

On the outskirts lay some church ruins resembling the landscape of a Clint Eastwood spaghetti western, a forlorn reminder of the lost era of Mexican bandits and gun-slinging heroes. The poverty of the people living in wooden shelters and dilapidated huts was disturbing, although some lived in flat concrete huts that had been built by foreign aid workers. We visited one such house, set high in the mountains. Outside, a group of bedraggled children sat watching our small party ascend the hill. They stared in dishevelled silence, suspiciously observing us. Outside one of the flat concrete buildings, a line of beautiful, hand-woven mats and shawls flapped a vibrant welcome. A small boy wearing a dirty shirt that was haphazardly buttoned hid behind a bright yellow mat. His beautiful face and pained dark eyes peeped at us shyly from behind his mother's handiwork, while his little sister sat having her hair plaited wearing her traditional costume. She smiled politely. Her mother turned away from the camera but allowed her little girl to have her picture taken.

On the dry, dusty ground a woman sat working a primitive loom. The main material was tied to a tree, and the other part was anchored around her waist. All the women wore long, black skirts and black, blue, or white tops designed with a strong regular pattern. All their clothes were homemade and hand-woven by them. The women displayed their handicrafts on an old straw mat, hoping we might buy something. The colours, so bold, bright, and vivid, were individual works of art.

Central America is known as "the Land of Colour." I was proud to buy a wall hanging of peacocks, birds, and flowers in vibrant blues, purples, reds, yellows, and greens. We were invited into the concrete dwelling followed by two of the children, who questioned us with their hostile eyes. I felt sorry for the little girl and gave her one of the bracelets I was wearing. She wore it and beamed, running out of the house, but seconds later, she appeared without it. I suspected one of the older children outside had commandeered her exotic trophy. Her sad eyes told all.

Inside the house, the bare, breeze-block walls gave cool shelter. The floor was a fine, pale silt dust, which was splattered with ash from the fire. A large grid was built up in the middle on a layer of bricks so that the fire could blaze under a large tortilla griddle. It was kept lit by planks of wood gathered from demolished wooden huts. It was hard to believe this was their living room! Bare walls, bare earth told of a meagre existence. A few old, black cooking pots lay next to the fire, with a dilapidated cement bucket for a water pot and coconut husks hewn out for bowls. On the rickety table covered by a bright red, hand-woven cloth were a few ears of corn. I recognised the yellow variety but was amazed to see white, black, and red. Also incongruous on the table was a Coca-Cola bottle and a white plastic bowl containing brown sugar. Three women knelt by the fire, patting the black corn dough into rough circles. Their fingers mingled with the dust from the floor as they placed the black tortillas onto the hot griddle. As the tortillas cooked, we were handed around a strange drink from a tin can. I only pretended to drink the infusion and, likewise, when the tortillas came round, I tore off only a small portion, as the texture and taste was like cardboard!

After our "snack," we were taken down the mountain to a larger village, where there was a time difference of half an hour; not for any specific reason, purely because the villagers deemed it so. The style of the villagers' costumes changed from geometric patterns in blues, blacks, and white to a more flamboyant style in greens, purples, and pinks, depicting floral and animal motifs. As we walked toward the village, women appeared from all directions to take up their places in the market stalls. The local handicraft work was wonderful, from beautifully knitted jumpers to fine lace blouses. I bought a jumper-jacket knitted in a typical Chiapas design with a long, pointed hood that had a tassel. The women were pleased with the group's purchases and cheered as we walked toward the main square. It was a major fiesta day, and everywhere, brightly coloured flags flapped in the breeze.

Ella and I entered a church heavily scented with burning incense. A group of men stood in the middle chanting, accompanied by a small Jewish harp type of instrument and a solitary drum. The men wore their traditional tunics, but on their feet

55

they wore strange, high platform sandals in which they danced primitively, stamping harshly in time with the drumbeat, adding a sharp clatter to the empty, hollow sound of the drum, which reverberated up to the high ornate ceiling. The Indian men had been chanting and stamping since the early hours of the morning. They smiled as they stepped back and forth in their simple dance, pleased to have an audience for a few moments. When we left them to their ritual, they acknowledged our leaving with a nod and a smile. We crossed to the next church, which was packed with most of the community, singing, wailing, praying, and chanting amid a thick smog of incense.

Ella was sucked into the atmosphere and was overcome with emotion. Tears softly trickled down her face. I held her hand, unaware at first of the presence of her husband standing next to me, but then I saw him, and we formed an electric channel of communication. I could see him plainly, his distinctive hair and electric blue eyes. Although I held her hand, it was really he who had taken my place, touching her, communicating with her while I safely removed myself to watch from outside my body. Miles away from the familiar, years away from normality in the Isthumus of Tehuantepec, three spirits fused. We stood, bathed in a cocoon of golden energy, surrounded by a bubble of light amid the flickering candles, festooned in the smell of wax and smoking incense, mingling with unwashed bodies wrapped in damp wool, a hint of honey and jasmine oil emanating from the women's hair.

Without words, the telepathic connection brought Ella close to the man she had loved and who had greatly suffered. There was so much left unsaid when he died that needed to be expressed between them, and I was honoured to be a channel for that purpose. As the chanting faded and the congregation shuffled, I came back from the distance, feeling light-headed. Holding hands, Ella and I slowly walked out into the bright sunshine, wiping away our tears.

9

007 Car Chase and Chicken Bus into Guatemala

Floating in a haze after the amazing experience in the church, we walked out into the blazing square, where the blaring, fiesta mariachi bands strummed their own unique brand of music, plucking at all kinds of homemade guitars and coaxing percussive instruments into sensuous Mexican rhythms. One of the musicians blew me a kiss from the bandstand, and I blew one back as I made my way to the van, hiding my camera from a group of Indians who did not like to be photographed.

Back in the van, I marvelled at the morning's events and was pleased for Ella to have found some inner peace. Back at San Cristobal, I spent time alone wandering around the shops, making sure that I noted landmarks to navigate my way back safely. I ate in a small restaurant, sampling the local tortillas, and I bought a lovely black amber ring in the shape of a teardrop. It symbolised an inner need to get rid of the sadness I had harboured from my last relationship and a celebration of the search for new adventures.

I made a special effort with makeup and hair, wearing my only pretty skirt, and both Ella and Maria complimented me on my appearance. I had travelled nonstop for days, wearing mostly jeans that I washed at night, so it was a lovely change to flaunt my femininity in my skirt. Our group split for the main meal, with the Complainers going off on their own; Maria, Ella, Gordon and I found a good restaurant before meeting up with everyone in a small pub with a live band. Terrino loved salsa dancing, and we cleared the small floor with our flash moves. Dancing was part of the culture, and no one felt shy or inhibited dancing with strangers. You didn't need language when you danced salsa.

A tall Mexican man wearing a white shirt, jeans, cowboy boots, and a Panama hat slinked across the bar. He looked distinguished and moved with confidence. I envisioned him as a ranch owner. He looked at me and moved forward with a smile. I glanced behind me to see who he was looking at and was surprised when he held out his hand to me. I accepted and enjoyed dancing a succession of numbers, but again, like Cinders, all too soon it was time to depart. He seemed sad, and so was I.

Back at the hotel, I began to feel unwell with stomach cramps. I feared being ill more than anything, and although I had special medicine for diarrhoea, I was scared to be debilitated or a burden on the group. I had a disturbed night but in the morning felt slightly better, avoiding breakfast just in case! After an early rise, we packed our bags into our little bus and were back on the road for a long, thirteen-hour journey. We had to cross the Guatemalan border, then board a local chicken bus to Lake Atitlan.

Terrino, always hungry, bought local food to eat on the bus. I couldn't bear to look at him and his greasy, spicy burger as we bounced up and down through the uneven potholes. Mile upon mile of untouched jungle spread before us, and spectacular, lush, green mountains fanned out against a cloudless cobalt sky. Hour after hour we wound up and down, in and around tropical rivers, snatching glimpses of golden Caribbean coastline.

Eventually, around midday, we approached the Guatemalan border and left our little bus by the side of the road. The heat devoured us, and I found it hard to breathe. We were high up in the mountains surrounded by thick vegetation, which camouflaged everything. For the first time on the journey, I felt unsafe. It would be simple to kidnap the group. It was a fact that Guatemala had the highest record in Central America of kidnapping and blackmailing foreigners. It would be so easy to lose a small group like ours! Through the dense thicket I sensed a watchful presence. The silence surrounding us was too heavy, almost oppressive. The business of leaving our bus and taking two local cars that appeared from nowhere, seemed shady. We were quickly bundled into the two dilapidated wrecks with a clandestine air of a secret mission. The drivers were nervous, not wanting to waste any time dawdling by the road. The interchange between Terrino and the men was suspicious. As I sat in the back ingesting the fumes that poured into the car, not only from ours but also from the one in front, my stomach began to curdle. The noxious vapour was making me nauseous, so I put my hands over my mouth and nose to stop inhaling the smoke.

Both cars clanged and banged their way up the steep incline. It was frightening to be on the edge of the precipice looking down as the road disappeared over the edge of the cliff. No one spoke. We clutched our bags to our chests in the hope of arriving safely at the Guatemalan border office. Perhaps Terrino was making a little money on the side by hiring two illegal cars instead of company taxis? Our driver scrunched his way through the rattling gearbox and managed to get us up the mountain and into a small town where the people were wary of us. We swung down a narrow alley into a marketplace but didn't stop; instead the driver increased speed! Terrified, we clung to one another, bouncing on the broken seats in the back, hitting the bottom of the road, then banging our heads against the battered roof. The grim race through the centre of the market accelerated as we fled from an invisible enemy, crashing into stands of vegetables and fruit, which tumbled across our wheels and splattered into other stalls. It was straight out of a James Bond movie, with all the thrills and spills of a highly choreographed car chase, and comical elements as young boys jumped out of our way and dove into other stalls, destroying small crates of livestock, smashing open imprisoned live birds. Escaped scrawny chickens flew into the windscreen squawking and clucking, and we could hear screams from the women who were laying out bales of beautiful cloth that sprang out of their hands, somersaulted across our path, and bounced back into the road, creating before us a gaily coloured pathway.

Our undercover entrance into the country was reckless and dangerous. The driver hurtled us through impossible territory, causing untold damage and disturbing the peace without a backward glance. Like a fairground ride when the inevitable black tunnel rises ahead and the unavoidable is only a sigh away, we hit the base of a steep hill with speed as the car exhaust, which hung by a thread like an infant's tooth, almost shot up through the bottom of the chassis. The car began to roll backward. I wanted to jump, but before we nearly crashed, people appeared from cracks in the wall, pulling and tugging us all the way up the hill. Sweat dripped down my back and hung in droplets from my chin as I mentally strained with every push up the uneven incline. My arms ached with the strain, my head thumped, and my stomach clawed through my gut, but there wasn't time to feel ill as we were rapidly bundled out of the car into the dry, dusty street, staring in disbelief as the two cars disappeared in a noisy sand cloud.

Terrino briskly whisked us into the border office to have our passports stamped and to obtain our visitors' passes. There was a fee to leave the Chiapas and a toll to enter Guatemala. As we stood in line to go in, the heat pounded down. I felt ill and uneasy. There was a strong sense of underground guerrilla support, with the shops on the opposite side of the road sporting full bandito gear, from black balaclavas and bandanas to camouflage shirts and trousers. Even the toy shop was full of play knives and instruments of war. All the dolls wore guerrilla gear; there wasn't one hint of a pink Barbie doll or sweet, pretty baubles for girls.

One by one, we stood with our bags in the dry, dusty road. There was no shelter from the sun. I stood in a cold sweat and began to shake, but as it was my turn next, there wasn't time to give in to my malady. The office was unimpressive, far from the adventurous world of espionage we had just escaped. A small, rotund official sat at his desk lazily shuffling forms and papers. Blue bottle flies buzzed hazily around his head. For him there was no hurry; in fact, he took pleasure in making us wait in the stillness of his lacklustre kingdom. Only the slow ticking of his wall clock interrupted his indifference. The smell of mold and stale tobacco cemented into the flaky walls polluted the visa card that he stamped and passed to me. Terrino spoke to him, persuading him to hurry so we could catch our chicken bus. A small bribe seemed to give him more purpose, and within a few minutes we all had the necessary papers to proceed on our journey. We were lucky, as a local chicken bus rounded the corner and Terrino urged us to hurry, telling us that sometimes passengers had had to wait hours before boarding.

I struggled up the hill, not feeling well. I had not eaten that day and found it hard to run with my rucksack. Henry, Mr. Complainer, saw my difficulty and took my rucksack and towed it up the hill with his. I was extremely grateful. Terrino said that we just had time to buy some food for the journey. By the side of the road local meat was being fried, but I couldn't face it, so I bought a bottle of lemonade and a packet of boiled sweets.

As we threw our bags in the back of the chicken bus, Terrino explained that the local buses obtained the name from carrying livestock but also the drivers played a game of "chicken" while driving up the steep roads through the mountains, racing each other along the narrow, precipitous ledges. Ella looked concerned for a moment, but I figured that nothing could be quite as hair-raising as the car chase we had just endured. Carrying my plastic bag with my beautiful poncho from Merida, I took a window seat and felt better after a few sips of lemonade. Everyone made fun of my plastic bag, but I had paid over the odds for the hand woven poncho and was not prepared for someone to take it from the baggage hold. Gordon looked ill and was suffering from back pain. I offered a little comfort by promising to work on his back when we reached Panajachel, a small town by Lake Atitlan.

The bus jogged along at an easy pace and the group spread out, having space to breathe after our hazardous journey, but after a couple of hours climbing up into the mountains, the bus began to fill up with local Indians returning from market, where they had bought live chickens and goods for the week. Almost every seat accommodated at least three people, squashed to capacity, and the aisle was crammed with bodies. When the bus filled up with more and more villagers, we were four to a tiny seat. One young woman with her baby and goods struggled, so I offered her my small space. She took it gratefully, with an embarrassed smile, but her baby, who had never seen a blonde, white woman before, was terrified of me and screamed, hiding his face in his mother's chest. His brother and sister laughed at his reaction. I tried to make friends, but it only made matters worse, as he howled with fright when I held out my hand. The other Indian women were amused but looked away politely. Squeezed up tightly against the women, I could smell unwashed bodies, sweet oil, unclean blankets, damp wool, and wet animals.

Throbbing, packed to the seams, the bus chugged up the mountainside, but as soon as another bus came alongside us, the race began. The driver, not heeding his passengers, thrust the bus into gear and started a manic burst forward, glancing sideways at his rival. The locals were used to this and took it as part of the ride, having every confidence in their mad driver to get them home safely. Everyone clung on tight as we neared a precipice and our driver, through sheer willpower, forced the other bus behind us. Our driver certainly was not chicken! We pushed ahead and won the race to the top. The locals smiled and the driver laughed. Gradually as we wove our way down the mountains, the bus stopped at intervals, delivering its passengers to their villages, until only our little gang was left in peace to spread out and breathe freely for the last part of the journey. The day had flung us from one hair-raising experience to another. Ella sighed with relief, exclaiming, "Well, I wouldn't have missed that for the world!"

As we pulled into Panajachel, there was a calm, peaceful air, yet the poverty was even more pronounced, with the local Indians banding together by Lake Atitlan to eek out a meagre existence. The light was soft, with an orange-pink tinge that hovered above the three imposing volcanoes surrounding the lakeside. Our accommodation was a series of rooms set in a compound in the middle of the town. A guard dog barked as we entered through the creaky gate. It was cheap and not very clean. The place gave the impression of an American gold-rush town, hastily set up and not completed, the main street lined with tin huts and wooden shacks with makeshift corrugated-iron roofs. Maria never complained, but I hated filth. Despite my upset stomach, I was very hungry, and the lemonade and sweets had helped to settle the churning. I decided it was time to take one of my two special tablets that would zap an infection so that I could enjoy the meal that Terrino had been arranged in a restaurant near the lakeside.

Our gang was tired and hungry after the long haul. The food was good and I spoilt myself with a gin and tonic. Everyone seemed relaxed and happy to have arrived safely. It was Friday; we had been travelling together as a group for one week. In this time we had fused into a unit, albeit a diverse one. My life back home seemed unreal; only my children anchored me to England. My quaint cottage in Yorkshire was but a distant memory. The person that had set out with a broken heart was finding new strength. In that moment, at that time, I was someone else, somewhere else, with a party, yet alone, sitting at a table enjoying the fading light as it bounced off Lake Atitlan, gradually piecing together the fragments of my cracked shell.

10

The Smoking Spanish Deity and Jesus

After the meal by Lake Atitlan, as promised, I went to Gordon and Ella's room to work on his back. He had travelled all day in pain over the rough terrain and suffered the car chase and chicken bus ride without a murmur, but the pain was written in his eyes. I did not ask to be a healer, it was the last thing I would have chosen; but after trying to avoid the gift, I accepted it, and I do the best I can for anyone who asks for help. Both he and Ella, after the strange experience in Palenque and our communication with Ella's deceased husband, believed in my ability. When the desire to heal is great and pure, the heat comes into my hands. I began to work on his back, feeling the electricity passing through me, forming into my hands then out into his back. I worked in a semi-trance for about half an hour, and then I left Gordon to absorb the energy.

Alone, I walked out into the cool evening air. A "Friday night out on the tiles" atmosphere was rising in the shantytown as I took the turning to the Chichi market leading down to the lake. The market was one long, uneven, cobble-strewn street lined by open wooden shacks; these were roofed with tarps, plastic, wood, and corrugated metal. Along the line of shops on either side were cafes and restaurants in similar shed style but open-fronted to the public with a few mismatched tables and chairs.

Parts of the street were muddy after the afternoon downpour with people hopping across the muddy puddles, I was reminded again of those spaghetti western movies. Blankets, clothes, bags, and shoes were set out enticingly, along with a feast of foods, making the walkway an explosion of colour and tantalizing smells. I loved the handmade cloth woven in the traditional patterns of each tribe, especially the blouses with intricate lace bodices, which must have taken hours of patient work. Handwoven cloth goods in a rainbow of colours, styles, and sizes were attractively laid out in the stalls. The market reached nearly all the way down to the lakeside but petered out near the rocky ledge marking the short distance between land and water.

In the dying light, as I reached the lapping waves, the sun was setting behind the volcano, streaking the sky with flashes of gold, red, and orange. Children watched me from a few paces, paddling in the cool water, somehow sensing not to pester me to buy their trinkets; instead they let me attend to my peace. I took time to listen to the gentle lapping of the waves against the craggy shore. It was a special time. My children's faces appeared on the surface of the darkening water. I needed to hug them. I wished I could share the beauty with them. A few stray tears tickled down my face. I was humbled and grateful to be in the love of that moment, realizing it was selfish of me to want more, to seek someone to love, when I had it all, knowing that many people around me had nothing.

Darkness came swiftly. Under the safe canopy of the silent volcanoes, self-pity had no place. The lure of the Chichi market was strong, and the evening was about to begin. I gave the children a little change as I strode back up the street and returned to the buzz of Friday night. The stalls were a treasure trove of exotic goods, both ancient and new. The local Indians were decked out in their tribal costumes selling fashionable skirts, trousers, and tops. It was a strange amalgam of cultures in a dark enclave lit by small fairground lights.

Lesley Ann Eden

I was inside a dreamscape in a secret place, both protected and threatened by the watching volcano gods. The handcrafted goods thrilled me and I wanted to buy everything, but I did not have the money or the space to carry them. Feeling adventurous, I was lured toward a tin-hut restaurant. The mud outside came inside the rough shelter, but no one seemed to mind. The night air was damp, harbouring the smell of sizzling onions, like a fairground maze of temptations. In my dreamscape, I was a lone character in my spaghetti western, wearing my grey, black, and white poncho from Merida. I entered the tin saloon deliberately and sat at a table in the middle of the sagging, wooden-slatted floor. From where I sat, I could see a tiny kitchenette with an old cooker and a cupboard. A waiter spied me and came over promptly to take my order. I felt daring in my movie and ordered a "whiskey e Sprite," basing myself on a mixture of Clint Eastwood and Mel Gibson from the Mad Max movies. Snug inside my scene, I watched the world outside as a cloudburst sent Indians, villagers, and tourists alike scattering to any available shelter. The mud increased, slithering and slopping on the rough floor as a crowd of people rushed inside.

To my amazement, the "crowd" was actually the band arriving. The lead guitar player owned the restaurant together with his Indian wife, who took charge of the cooking. They had a small son who sat by the drummer playing his own imaginary drum kit with two knives beating the wooden table. It was a bizarre scene. The band was made up of middle-aged musicians, all male except for a tall woman with white hair who was the percussionist. I imagined she must have been quite stunning when she was younger. She would not have been out of place in an office taking dictation from the boss instead of in my little Klondike scene where she swayed graciously in her trousers and white blouse, tapping, ticking, scraping, and shaking when the music demanded. When the band struck up one of my favourite Santana pieces, "Black Magic Woman," I was miraculously transported out beyond the tin roof to a concert hall among the stars. The music was brilliant. It was hard to believe that in a little shanty shack by Lake Atitlan, thousands of miles from home,

I could be entranced, hypnotically lost in live music played by gifted musicians. I closed my eyes, internally dancing the beats and didn't see Ella and Gordon enter; only when they took the seats beside me did I notice Gordon's smile and see him sitting with ease and no sign of pain. They ordered drinks, and I had another whiskey and Sprite, indulging my saloon scene to the full. I was surprised to see dishes appear on the tables from the tiny closet kitchen— Spanish tortillas, Italian pizzas, and Thai curries! Magically, from a tiny stove in a cupboard, the most elegant and exotic cuisine was conjured.

I stayed rapt in the music for a few hours, not able to drag myself away, but when the effects of the whiskey, the medication, and the long travel haul kicked in, I slithered back through the mud to the compound where the dog was tethered to a stake in the middle of garden barking at all the new visitors. I slumped onto the small bed, being careful not to look at the filthy floor, and slid between the clean sheets. Maria was out and the night closed in on my movie.

I always woke up before Maria, and would creep by her to take a shower. We had an early start this morning to catch the boat for a trip around Lake Atitlan. I woke Maria and slipped out into the early morning where only a few cafes were open. I found a small restaurant at the top of the Chichi Market. It was beautifully decorated with exotic flowers that smelt fresh and delicate. I was hungry and dared to eat a full breakfast but avoided the sloppy brown beans. Ava and Henry also appeared with Gordon and Ella, who seemed pleased to have discovered the lovely place. The previous day had been a huge push across the border down into Guatemala, but two nights in Panajachel would give us chance to recover. Saturday was our day for the gentle boat ride around Lake Atitlan, visiting little islands nestled around it.

I was always amazed at how Maria just appeared on time for everything, miraculously managing to grab a hot croissant from a nearby vendor before jumping into the small boat. The sun was already hot as we glided under the watchful eye of the awesome volcanoes out across the azure stretch of peaceful water under the heavenly clear sky. The air was pure. The lush vegetation, glistening with morning dew, shaded the island villages so that only the high church steeple was visible from the top of San Antonio. As we drew up into the tiny harbour alongside small wooden fishing boats lined full of empty corn husks, children came running down to the rickety wooden jetty to greet us. Foreigners meant money and a means to supporting a meagre, poverty-stricken existence. San Antonio had a cooperative shop next to the school, where the children made lovely little models of chicken buses and birds and the women made hand-woven bags in which to sell their home-grown coffee and crocheted hats and scarves. I bought coffee and a little model of a chicken bus, which had a variety of fruit balanced on the top.

Outside, a tiny child stood forlornly with a tray of friendship bracelets and stared up at me with pained dark eyes. She was perhaps three years old. My heart ached to help her, so I bought a handful of bracelets. Poverty was reflected in her helpless little face as she allowed me to take her picture with the expectation of a few more coins. From an older child further up the hill I bought some worry dolls in a tiny woven bag. As I ventured even further up the winding streets, the women came out of their houses with welcome smiles while lazy dogs cocked their heads to one side wondering whether to make the effort to bark. But it was too hot for them. August was a month of extreme heat and heavy rainfall, the perfect mixture for hurricanes, and a dangerous one was forecast!

I was out of breath at the top of the hill where the Church of San Antonio proudly stood, erected by the locals and Catholic missionaries. A group of women gossiped outside, dressed in their traditional Indian costume. One of them ventured to talk to me. She spoke softly in Spanish, asking for my beautiful crystal earrings. I was amazed at her daring but declined graciously and gave her my lovely bracelet. In return she gave me a ribbon she had woven. She was interested to know about my children and learn about the outside world. She was fascinated by my independence and way of life, as she was a wife and mother and, as such, had limited freedom in her small social world.

I wished I had more time to spend with her and learn about her lifestyle, but time was running out and I needed to buy batteries for my camera. I found some in an old, dusty store but of as soon as I put them in my camera they went dead. Near the harbour a woman, gaily dressed in her traditional costume, caught me unawares and began to braid my hair with a huge length of thin, hand-woven ribbon. She plaited my hair in the style of the village women. I didn't protest and allowed her to finish her handicraft. I liked what she did with my hair, and it was worth the small amount of money to have the experience.

Back on the boat, the sun's rays were more intense and my exposed neck got burnt. Ava kindly applied sunscreen, but I could feel my skin already blistering. The next island, San Jose, was a short distance away, and as we drew up to dock, I spied an impressive lineup of chicken buses, all polished and gleaming in the sunlight. We trekked up to a large, open quadrangle where a school had been built. Terrino explained that we were about to visit the local deity, Maximon, who was a god mixed from Mayan and Spanish beliefs. He told us how the villagers took turns hosting the deity in their houses for six months at a time, and in return, they received all manner of gifts and money. I had no idea what was waiting for us!

We followed Terrino quietly up the steep slope toward a clutch of wooden huts that resembled the chicken house my Grandmother had kept when I was a child. I soon realised with horror that the huts were homes, and, as we ducked under some protective plastic covering, to my disbelief, we entered the inner world of the villagers. Inside the maze of clutter it smelt like my grandmother's chicken house and even looked like it! Pots and pans were scattered under makeshift shelves on the dusty floor. It was hard to believe that people lived in such dire poverty. Large families were crammed inside the battered huts, existing without kitchen or bathroom. We tramped through the dim enclosure toward a henhouse, where we climbed up a few wooden steps before entering a dark room. There was a large, old wooden table in the middle and four wooden benches. It was a few seconds before my eyes became adjusted to the murky light, and I could just make out a figure balanced on the table that resembled a scarecrow, a puppet, and a stuffed Guy Fawkes effigy.

In the gloom, three men sat opposite our small party. One lit a candle, the yellow glow exposing craggy faces appearing like three sly bandits waiting to rob a bank. I turned my head to the left and was stunned to find next to me an ornate glass coffin carved with dark, polished wood around the rim. A man with eyes open wide to heaven was inside. A rush of sick stuck in my throat, and I had to swallow hard to push it back down to the pit of my stomach. I was terrified. I gulped and took a deep breath. I was stunned to be sitting next to a dead man in a coffin. I dared to snatch another brief look; to my relief, it was a life-size statue of Jesus, so realistic and lifelike with living flesh tones that, in the shadowy gloom, it appeared human.

In the eerie murkiness, one of the old men began to talk softly about Maximon. He pointed to a small ladder leading up to the loft where the effigy was put "to sleep" at night. I had a flashing vision of it being thrown up carelessly into the attic as the men laughed mockingly. Another man told us that Maximon was highly revered and visitors came from far and near to hear his wisdom and give people advice about many things. In return they always left gifts, which were displayed on the table: cigarettes, radios, mobile phones, all kinds of things were pointed out to us and, of course, money was donated! Another man picked a cigarette up off the table, lit it, and then put it into the dummy's mouth. Miraculously the effigy smoked it, puffing out coils of grey cloud into the ominous atmosphere. We were supposed to be stunned by this miracle, being a sign and proof of Maxomon's living power. We were invited to consult the oracle, but no one volunteered a question. An uncomfortable silence hung in the shadows as the slim candle flickered, throwing a strange light on Jesus in his coffin. The charade, where the men were playing their life out on a stage of deceit, did not impress me.

Strange happenings had been part of life since I could walk, but trickery was only trickery. Just before I went to school, at nearly five years old, my younger brother and I devised unusual games, one of which gave us many hours of delight. We discovered it by mistake one day when we were playing hide-and-seek and I was under the bedcovers while my brother hid. Unfortunately, I could see through the covers and knew exactly where he was hiding. He was surprised when I found him immediately and wanted to know how I did it. I told him I could see. He didn't believe me, so we did a test. I went under the covers again, and he piled on top all the toys he could find, and hid again. But I could still see! We tested my ability further by hiding in cupboards, which I could see through, by blindfolding me and hiding in wardrobes. It didn't make any difference; I could still see through matter. We played the game for a while, but when I went to school, everything changed; he was my baby brother, and I was busy learning new, important, grown-up things, like writing my name. We no longer played that game, and my ability to see through matter disappeared.

It was strange to be part of three worlds—the ancient Spanish deity offering the villagers hope; the Christian God forced onto the people by the missionaries to bring salvation to the heathens and the modern technological world of mobile phones and computers lying static on the weathered table—all converged into a hen hut. Looking closer at the Jesus statue, my Catholic childhood flooded back, along with everything I detested about the oppressive, abusive distortion, spawned in the name of Love, under the banner of Rome. I was relieved to have rejected the brain-washing catechism beaten into me and was sickened to see the same bleeding heart open to save the world in a tiny, out-of-the-way chicken scoop somewhere in the Guatemalan jungle.

Catholicism was my mother's salvation. I had been happy attending my tiny village school surrounded by trees and fields, but when I turned nine, my mother's conscience dictated that I go to a Catholic school in the next town, a dark old building with no windows to let in the sunshine, no trees, the rank stench of stale beer from pubs hanging in the grimy air first thing in the morning as I raced through the town to get to school on time or risk caning in front of everyone!

I was an outcast from the first day. I had no uniform. I had long, plaited hair and wore glasses. I was different. I used my gifts to outwit the children who set traps for me in the classroom. They didn't know that I could see what they were doing without looking at them. They were amazed that I knew to step over cotton tied across desks, to jump over dog messes placed strategically, that I could outrun and outclimb the boys. The headmistress, a nun who was keen on football and sport, saw my ability to sprint and set me to race for the school, where I created new records. The cruel deputy headmistress learnt of my ability to play the piano, so I played for the class's singing lesson. Through my skills I won my classmates' respect, so I didn't have to use my psychic energy to survive.

In the dark chicken hut, I had no empathy with the deity, but I did leave a little money. Our money was gratefully received by the smoking deity, which managed to puff out more smoke as we placed our offerings on the table in front of him. Eagerly we scrambled out of the hut into the dim light of the chicken-run world and made our way back down the mountain to visit the next island, San Marco.

Back in the boat the sun, in a cloudless sky, blazed directly onto the lake, and Ava offered to put more sunscreen onto my blistering neck. She and Henry had, as always, extensive information about all the islands, and they told me that San Marco was special in that it ran all kinds of courses, and gave psychic respite and directional advice to people exploring a spiritual path. A vision of me sitting at my computer at school on a grey, foggy morning as "Creative Writing in Guatemala" flashed across my screen, jerked my memory. I wondered if San Marco was the island that had first tempted me to seek an adventure. Ava gave me the tourist guidebook and, from reading the blurb, I was surprised to see that it was the very same. Gently riding the undulating waves in the middle of Lake Atitlan, on a Saturday morning, in a world far from York, was strange, especially gliding along on a small boat to a place that had stirred up my need for adventure in the first place.

As we disembarked from the boat, we were engulfed by lush, paradisiacal plants. The island was a beautiful Garden of Eden set under powerful volcanoes. I hung back from the rest of the group as they trekked up to the house to view the meditation centre and mock pyramid. A false vibration disturbed me. I was glad I had not booked the course. Something had veered me away toward a completely different adventure. I did not see anyone from the centre and wandered in and out of the dense overgrowth with an overriding sense of fake spirituality. Having been a hippie in my youth, the place wreaked of bogus "flower power" and middle-class trendies. Perhaps it was a harsh judgment—many people might derive spiritual guidance from the place—but for me, it was a phony set-up.

I ventured back toward the boat and took a detour by a strange house that had a tree growing out of it. As I drew nearer, I realised that it was a small shop and that the tree protruded out through the middle of it. A small boy, about six years old, sat by the door, engrossed in drawing a picture. I asked if I could take a photograph of him and the amazing tree, but he said in a sweet, soft voice, "No, no photograph of me, but take one of my homework." I wanted to laugh but refrained, as he was deadly serious. So I did as he wished. He had a teacher who came regularly to the island who set him tasks that he undertook with pride. He was proud to be educated, which was far removed from the unruly, loud-mouthed, rude teenagers I taught back home.

We didn't stay long on the island as we had a lunch date at the next island a few minutes away. There we found a completely different setting, one akin to a small Cornish fishing village. It seemed as though we were alighting to a country cottage ablaze with bright flowers, fresh, verdant grass, and herb gardens. I lovingly ran my hands through the lavender bushes and breathed in the clean, sweet fragrance that could calm a troubled mind and relax a tired soul. I scrunched a leaf of mint in my fingers, rubbing the balmy juice in my hands, remembering mint sauce and Sunday roasts, Yorkshire puddings and thick, meaty gravy.

We were greeted by a young Irish couple who were running the hotel for the absent owner. They showed us to a lovely feast set out in the shade by a rockery. We were quite hungry after an early start and quickly tucked into the spread of assorted salads, cold meats, and cheese. I wanted to eat, but a sharp pain in my stomach reminded me that infection was bubbling, so I dared to swallow only soup and bread. I was tempted by the fruit and succumbed, knowing it was a mistake, and I paid for my greed a few minutes later. My head ached, I felt dizzy, and my blistered neck stung. I wished I could enjoy the beautiful oasis and relax in the bizarrely English setting, listening to our hosts' soft Irish lilt, out of place with our location. But all I could think of was getting back to the squalid hotel to take some medicine.

We took an hour for lunch and then set back on the boat to Panajachel, where the Saturday market was heaving. I quickly made my way back to the compound, where the crazy dog tugged at his chain in the centre of the dry grass and barked at everyone passing. I had taken one of my two special pills for traveller's stomach and decided that I would battle on and leave the last one for a dire emergency. I slept for a while and woke when the sun was setting, feeling better but cramped with hunger pangs. I decided to revisit the tin-hut restaurant in the hope that the band would return.

As I made my way down the market, I was reminded of Saturday night in York, where punters attempt to visit every pub on the Micklegate run, and as each tin hut oozed a boozy welcome, it was tempting to try each one. However, I resisted the call and entered my favourite hut. The waiter recognised me, asking if I wanted a whiskey y Sprite. I nodded and ordered a paella from the menu. I was amazed when a huge dish appeared from the tiny kitchen cupboard. It was delicious. Halfway through my meal I was delighted when the band appeared. I watched them set up their instruments in the tiny space next to the broken lavatory. It was amusing to squeeze through the band while they were playing to go to the toilet, but I had to remind myself that this was the Klondike and I should be grateful for even a primitive amenity.

The musicians smiled, recognising me from the previous night. Before they began their concert, I bought one of their CDs, heaping great praise on their playing. I still couldn't comprehend how musicians of their calibre were making music in a ramshackle hut in the middle of nowhere. The thrill of the songs was the same as the previous night, and I drifted with the rhythm out to another planet, escaping my aching stomach and travel weariness. The sound connected me to my dance school, and I thought of all the wonderful children who took classes with me and how we had all become part of one big family, together with my own children. In my performing arts school, we continuously strove for better shows with more unusual effects through strange choreography. Whenever I would return from my travels, I was inspired by my experiences to teach children with music from different cultures and give them new steps I had learnt from people in far-off lands. As I sat there holding the CD, I knew I would play the songs for the children in York, which seemed, at that moment, so far away.

I afforded myself two more whiskies, convincing myself that it was medicinal, and drifted blissfully into my own world where the music was all. Sitting alone among the crowd, I was glad to be part of a unique experience, but, whether in York or the wilds of Guatemala, Saturday night when you're alone is the loneliest night of the week!

II

Chicastenango and Salsa with Blue Feet

What is the now?
Bleak Sunday.

It is January. Christmas and New Year festivities have faded. I had a wish to have all of my children and grandchildren under my roof for just one night, and my wish was granted. It was wonderful to cluck over my chicks amidst their bellyaching laughter, with a few stray tears, but above all to share our closeness. I have stored the memory.

The now is miserable. I am in bed with the flu. The rims of my eyes are raw. My head throbs in a puffed cotton-wool fever, and my teeth ache. I peer at the monochrome grey, watery sky and am glad it is the only Sunday in months when I am not rehearsing. My little puppy dog does not understand why I am in bed when I should be up chasing him. His eyes are full of love as he snuggles his head next to me. I cover my head, but he grips the sheets with his teeth. I burrow down under the quilt, but he scrabbles at the duvet as though he is discovering one of his buried bones. Excitedly, he finds me, licking my face with gusto. I have to get up; he won't let me lie in misery. The kitchen is cold. I snuggle my dressing gown around me as I sip tasteless coffee, remembering the Sunday when I prepared to leave Panajachel to travel to Chichicastenango market in the Guatemalan highlands . . .

I walked out into the early morning sun. The compound was quiet. The dog was nowhere to be seen, only his chain lay abandoned on the patchy grass. I asked a cleaner where he was. She shrugged her shoulders and said," Dog mad! He dead!"

I was shocked at the idea of having a rabid dog in the compound. I had chosen to have the anti-rabies injection, but it only allowed twenty-four hours to get to a hospital before the bite became fatal. The dog could easily have broken loose and bitten someone! I shuddered, remembering the documentary of a rabid woman in her last moments; her mad eyes still torment me. I was relieved to get back on the bus and travel through the Guatemalan highlands to one of the oldest markets in the world.

The tiny roads were quiet, as most of the farmers rested on Sundays, and we wound in and around the villages unimpeded by farm vehicles. As we passed the small outposts, we saw groups of Indians gathered by the isolated churches, where they placed fresh-cut flowers at the feet of statues of Mary and Jesus. Inasmuch as Christianity was apparent, the ancient religion of the Maya, with its ingrained superstitions, was still an obviously integral part of the Indians' culture. Icons of Mayan gods hung side-by-side with the bleeding Jesus and the Virgin Mary.

When we arrived, the town was already full of tourists mingling with the locals from the surrounding mountain villages, ready to sell, barter, and buy their way through the morning. We were taken to a quaint hotel full of beautiful parrots, in all the colours of the rainbow, squawking freely from their perches around the garden and verandas. An old Indian sat on the floor in the middle of an open quadrangle playing a strange instrument that resembled a glockenspiel–cum-gamelan. Three notes of the instrument reverberated throughout the hotel at the same frequency and in a continuous rhythm, monotonously droning a dirge. It was invasive—it even resounded in the lavatory.

After our comfort visit to the hotel, Terrino lead us out to the main square, which was dominated by a church and a market. The steps leading up to the church were crowded with groups of people selling flowers and religious icons, and the poorest Indians attempted to sell decaying fruit. Incense leaked through the church doors out into the masses and almost overwhelmed us with its heaviness as we entered the church's dark portals. Rows of eyes stared at our small party as we came in. I didn't like the oppressive atmosphere and walked out into the bright sunshine. Two Indian women slaughtered a chicken in the middle of the market, and the blood splattered onto the ancient cobbles as the "Kyrie Eleison" echoed from the church. Two differing religious customs blended into the market stalls.

Ava appeared through the crowd, victoriously waving her purchases. She was so good at haggling, too adept at beating down the locals to almost nothing. I picked up a beautiful wall hanging, which must have taken hours of hand sewing, and admired it. The Indian woman selling it offered me a price which was too high, so I walked away, but the woman ran after me, as it was considered an insult to her work not to sell it. Ava intervened and knocked her price right down. I felt guilty, but the woman seemed happy and smiled as she handed it to me.

The market was heaving with tourists and it was difficult to squeeze through the masses. I kept my purse close to my chest, as thieving was rife and so easy in the thick throng. The local Indians were as curious about us as we were about them. We brought a strange, alien world of materialism into their rural, poverty-stricken community, with our sunburnt faces, gold watches, bright red lipstick, and lascivious tongues, judging all by our Western standards. I loved the market but hated the smugness of the triumphant European exultant in his haggling, sporting three cameras with an extended lens that dug into everyone's backs in the crowd. I was relieved to scrabble back to the main road to wait for the bus.

It was uncomfortably hot standing in the sunshine with the dry dust catching in the back of my throat. My stomach began to rumble, with hints of the infection erupting. Water and more water was the answer to dehydration sickness, but it didn't help the bowel bug situation when facilities were scarce. Travelling seemed one long endurance test, using a minimum amount of effort to meet the extremes of discomfort. I had wanted to take myself out of my comfort zone, had wanted to be tested, had wanted to take the lid off my brain to see what was inside, had wanted to step off the edge of the universe alone, but now, standing in the burning heat of the midday sun, not able to share my fears with anyone, was hard. Ella had said, "Make a friend of loneliness," but it was not easy.

The bus was late, and waiting for it in the raw heat had made everyone irritable as we clambered in wearily. The Complainers complained about the seating on the bus, but they already had taken the best seats at the front. Ella, Gordon, and I sat at the back, where the rolling, bumping, and rocking in and out of potholes was awful, but we didn't complain. Maria kicked her feet in the dust, and Gunte leaned against a wall with a bored look. They had sat together for the first time during the journey to the market, and we were all hoping that a little friendship might blossom between them, but in the stark moment, they preferred their separate space. The drive to the forest restaurant was not long, and after only an hour's drive, we arrived at a lovely place. A straggle of hungry Indian children hung by the roadside, and Ella and Gordon made sure they had something to eat.

Inside was clean and airy, with two little Indian maids cooking tortillas over an open grill. A glockenspiel band played merrily at the back of the room. Ordering our food in the civilised cool of the dining room had restored our good humour, and everyone settled down to enjoy the experience. We ate and drank well, ordering unusual drinks, but little did Ella and I know that the drinks would upset us both.

The atmosphere reminded me of the time when I worked in Spain and lived in a hotel by the sea, where every Sunday the locals would fill the hotel from lunchtime to late evening. It was their special family day. In the restaurant the same ambience pervaded the room, with smartly dressed waiters and waitresses preparing for the Sunday invasion.

A couple of hours later, we were back on the road, making our way through the Guatemalan highlands to the colonial town of Antigua, which was once the third largest city in all of Spanish America. Terrino, who perpetually had food on hand, told us that Antigua was Guatemala's capital city for two hundred years before it was destroyed by an earthquake in 1773. Munching on a bag of local mixed nuts, he explained that we could ride horses up one of the volcanoes and view the city from the top. Everyone seemed excited by that idea, but I doubted my leg's ability to cope with the strain, not to mention I did not have the money to do so. I was more interested in taking salsa lessons with a fantastic teacher, and even though I couldn't walk up volcanoes, I could still dance! Maria was excited by the thought, however, and pressed Terrino for more details.

When we arrived in Antigua, it was damp and misty, wrapped in an eerie silence of Sunday reverence. For the first time, it was necessary to wear a cagoule as we tramped through the cobbled streets to our small guesthouse. Inside was convent-like, with a series of small rooms built around an open courtyard. The doors were dark mahogany, beautifully carved and heavily embossed, giving an air of broody foreboding. Maria and I were to share a very basic room, but it had a clean, neat bathroom. I imagined that it had been scrubbed by nuns at prayer repeating the rosary. We were to spend three nights in Antigua, which was sheer luxury as we were continually on the move; time for me to come to grips with my washing!

After sorting out a few things, I went with Ella and Gordon to explore the area and get a cup of coffee. I was under a wave of depression in the foggy afternoon, without reason. We found a respectable café in the centre that had a xylophone band playing enthusiastically in the entrance hall. It was a replica of Yorkshire's Betty Cafés, waitresses dressed in black with little white, frilly aprons and headbands, waiting efficiently carrying large trays of elaborate cakes to the tables. I forced conversation, but I didn't really feel like communicating. The coffee was fine and the cake not as exciting as it looked. When we finished, I thanked Gordon and Ella for their company, but I needed to be alone, so I went out to explore the streets. Terrino had told us where the bank was, and I made my way to the main square and found it easily, making continuous spot checks after my scary experience in Merida, especially as the city was built on a grid and all the streets looked the same, with single-story houses built in lines along ancient cobbled streets. The curbs were unusually high to cope with the torrential downpour each afternoon, as the drainage system was primitive and caused mini rivers to rise from nowhere that subsided into tiny rivulets by early evening.

In the square, groups of dishevelled people gathered, drinking whatever they could to soften the blow of their reality, while proud Indians and their children from different regions paraded in their multicoloured, hand-woven ponchos. I met Maria in the square, and we decided to go for a drink. The mist cleared, forcing steam to rise from the ancient cobbles in the fresh afternoon air as the sun beat down mercilessly. In the brightness, my depression lifted as we ambled past a mustard-colored stone church.

We found a pleasant bar, and I ordered a whisky in the hope of culling my gut infection. We spent a pleasant couple of hours before meandering back. I was glad to be with Maria, as the streets were more confusing than I had first perceived. Back at the pensione, a few more visitors had arrived, and their chatter livened up the dim corridors. The rains had washed the inner square, leaving droplets of water glistening on the foliage as I sat under the canopy of lush palms. The dying rays of the tropical sun splayed intricate shadows on the courtyard walls. I kicked off my battered blue shoes, revealing my ugly stained feet, and noticed a collection of unusual, small, grey boulders. Without my spectacles, I couldn't make out the interesting patterns embossed in the grain. I closed my eyes for a few seconds, enjoying the dying sun on my face, but when I opened my eyes again, I was certain the boulders had moved. I thought I must have imagined it and returned to my nap, but a movement near my toes made me jump. The boulders had moved and, as I peered closely at them, a little head thrust out of a turtle shell! I was shocked but also glad I hadn't rested my feet on one! The troupe of turtles was closing in on me, and although they were not likely to bite, I moved to the library to read a book to wait for our group meeting.

As everyone gathered, it was obvious that the Complainers had ostracized themselves from the rest of the group. On the one hand, I admired them for their individuality, but on the other, the nature of the trip required getting on in a group and making compromises. Terrino gave us a choice about taking a small aircraft to get to Flores, a small island off Lake Peten Itza. We could continue in our little bus, but to give us more time on Flores, we could catch a midget army aircraft for a small fee. Everyone agreed to this idea, but I didn't say anything, I was prepared to use some of my allowance to accommodate the group's wishes. The rest of the meeting was taken up with people booking their various excursions for the next day. As usual I intended to wander alone exploring the city. Maria was excited about riding a horse up the volcano.

Just as I was returning back to my room, Gordon took me to one side and said, "I noticed that you didn't say anything in the meeting." I told him there wasn't anything to say.

"You agreed to go on the plane though?"

I nodded.

"That was a lovely thing to do", he said, "when I know you can't afford it!"

I hung my head, embarrassed by his words. He thrust some notes into my hand and walked back down the corridor. I didn't know what to say. His generosity was overpowering, and I was so grateful. His gift helped me more than I could tell him.

That evening we all ate together in a lovely restaurant and, as usual, Terrino made us all wait while he tucked heartily into his starter; the Complainers ordered their usual bottle of wine; Gunte, influenced by Terrino, hit the larger; Maria was not a drinker, while Gordon, Ella, and I each had a modest glass of wine. Ella's stomach, after the meal in the forest restaurant, was not well, and mine was equally unsettled, so we chose the least spicy food. Terrino said that we must all visit the infamous Irish bar in the city centre where all Brits met up for a drink.

It was peculiar walking into the bar with predominantly British people drinking Guinness, speaking English with accents from all over the country—Scotland, Ireland, Newcastle, and

Yorkshire! It was a taste of home in the middle of a tropical city. It was odd to be able to understand everyone's conversation and feel an affinity with the crowd. Drinking a gin and tonic in the heat of the night with old jokes drifting across the bar made me realise how bizarre the scene was, especially with some of the local Indians sitting on the pavement outside, gazing into the bright lights.

Suddenly my stomach twisted in a knot. I needed to find the toilet quickly! I raced up the stairs to find a small, dilapidated room whose red paint was peeling off its graffiti-ridden walls. I reached there just in time. The room spun, my head throbbed, my body broke out in a cold sweat. For a few minutes, the whole world erupted, and I was left shaking. There was no water to wash my hands! I tried flushing the toilet, but nothing worked. There was nothing to clean the lavatory with! I had no choice but to leave the loo in a terrible state. I rushed back down the stairs feeling like a criminal, hoping no one would go in after me. I took my half-full glass and poured the contents onto my hands. No one noticed in the crowded bar, and the dirty wooden floor rapidly drank in the spilt liquor. At least my hands felt clean! I needed to get out of the bar into the night air. The Indians stared as I hastened past them. I needed to get back to the guesthouse and wash.

Exhausted, I lay down to sleep. The sheets were clean, but I couldn't rid myself of the fear of long-legged creatures crawling out of the old wooden ceiling and creeping over my sleeping body. I dreaded being disadvantaged by traveller's stomach and closed my eyes, slipping into a deep, black void. Often when I am really ill, my special energy colours come to me. The most powerful healing colour is pinkish-purple, and if I need extra powerful energy, it has a blood-red centre. The energy mass is a swirling membrane of kaleidoscopic, amoebalike gyrations that slowly enfold me. There are different-coloured entities for different purposes, but mostly it is the purple plasm that comes to my aid. Deep inside the amethyst cavern, I am lost. I do not remember what happens, only that I emerge feeling better when the spirit mass dissipates.

The next morning, everyone left to climb the volcano and I wandered in the city centre in search of breakfast. I found a clean café and ordered a simple egg on toast with coffee and a fresh mango drink. I had taken antidiarrhoea tablets, not wishing to use my antibiotic medicine, as I still had a long way to travel. In the bright morning sunshine, I meandered along the main shopping street and was amazed to find an open-fronted store displaying expensive, elaborate beds, bedding, and bedroom furniture. I gazed at the beautifully designed interior and wondered how these people could afford such luxury. I was in awe of the quality and majesty of the scene; I imagined how the local Indians must have felt peering into a dream which they could never afford.

I wandered further down the street into a craft bazaar and admired the local art and the rough woven cloth. At the back of the long store, about twenty Moximon effigies glared down at me! I had no doubt that they could all smoke a cigarette just like the one we were supposed to revere in the mountains. What a revelation! Moximon was sold as a commodity! I stared at all the carved wooden faces with the high cheekbones and the gaping mouth from which the smoke "miraculously" bellowed. The style of costume was essentially the same. I smiled knowingly as I passed them and wondered what fun it would be to take one home if I had had the money and the space!

I spent the day wandering all over the city and shuddered when I passed the Irish bar, hoping the mess had been cleaned. I didn't dare to go in but I did meet a group of girls outside the bar. One was from York! She was distressed and told me that she had arrived on a sponsored trip to help build houses for the poor Guatemalan people in the hills, but the four of them had been held at gunpoint and had had all their money and passports stolen . They were amazed at my daring to wander alone, but it hadn't occurred to me to be afraid, as I had spent many years of my life travelling solo. The police had an idea who had their money, but he hadn't been found.

As I left them, they seemed confident that they would be helped but were apprehensive about my safety after their awful ordeal. I sauntered back to the pensione; if I were held at gun-point I would have to deal with it, but I was too tired to worry, so I slept for while but was woken by a troubled Maria, who was shaking with anger as she tearfully flopped down on her bed.

" I 'ate dem, I 'ate dem, 'orrible people!" She sobbed in her deep Italian accent.

I went and sat next to her, soothing her hair, coaxing her to explain.

"I ordered my 'orse, and dey took mine. Dey 'adn't ordered any, and dey snatched mine! Dey didn't listen to de guide! Dey rode off by demselves! Dey were told not to go beyond de ridge, but dey did, dey did! She looked so stupid; stupid little woman in little silver shoes! And de guide, he told her, he 'ad never seen anyone go up de volcano in silver slippers!"

She didn't even have to explain who "dey" were; I instinc-tively knew and imagined the scene. The Complainers had over-stepped the mark. Gordon and Ella also complained about their selfish, dangerous behaviour, and it was agreed to formalise a complaint to Terrino, who arranged a special meeting with them in the library. No one knew what was said, but they seemed slightly better afterward. From that moment, Maria never again spoke to them directly. If she had to, it was in a curt, impolite manner, even refusing to sit opposite them or look at them, which made matters a little uncomfortable at times!

We had a salsa lesson booked for that evening, and Maria, having recovered from her outburst, was hungry. As we walked with Gunte through the busy evening streets, she saw a dismal kiosk where a young girl was about to light a dirty grill in front of an open window. Maria ordered a barbequed chicken sand-wich. I watched with horror as the girl took a piece of charred chicken out of a plastic tub with her bare hands and began to reheat it over the grease-encased grill. From an old tin bin, she took some bread and smeared it with salsa sauce from a dusty jar. Using a pair of oily black tongs, she placed the rubbery chicken inside the bread and handed it to Maria, wiping her hands on her soiled apron. Maria took it gratefully and munched happily all the way down the flooded street. I momentarily put

Lesley Ann Eden

my hand along her shoulder, feeling gentle heat rise through my palm, secretly implanting protective energy, as I feared she might become ill from the impromptu snack.

I was nervous and excited about the lesson. Always as a dancer, there is the fear that a set of steps may prove too difficult to master. I didn't want to look silly in front of Maria and Gunte. As we entered the minute studio, the heat of the night followed us and ensnared us in the tiny space. Even with a small fan blaring out a pittance of a cool breeze, it was like an oven. The teacher, Miguel, was small, with oily, strong, muscled arms, handsome dark features, and a winning smile. In his black T-shirt and trousers, he could have stepped out of the *Dirty Dancing* film, as he deftly demonstrated the first few steps. Luckily I picked them up easily, and he immediately commented on my style. Maria told him that I was a dancer, and he nodded in recognition of my ability, which was both a relief and a joy, especially when he spent some time with me on more complicated steps. I tried not to look at my feet in the mirror as I was embarrassed by the blue dye, which, instead of fading with time, had engrained itself deeper into my white feet. My scruffy blue sandals never dried out in the rainy season, consequently my feet were always wet, except in bed!

Maria coped, and so did Gunte, but for me, the lesson was over too quickly and, as we made our way to the battleground of the salsa club, my poor blue feet squelched with sweat and more rain. I had thought that the lesson was over, but the rhythm of the night had just begun, and, as we entered the Latino bar, I realised that salsa was a serious business. The men fought passionately through their dance. Couples twisted tirelessly, flicking legs and arms spuriously, gyrating hips and thighs teasingly, while slinking backward and forward sexily through the crowded dance floor. I had not realised how the men paraded like peacocks and flaunted their individual steps, using the women as their steeds to transport them all over the stage, vying for the best spot in the limelight.

My teacher had said that it was the job of the male to show off his female partner, but each male displayed his own specialty under the spotlight, fighting to be hailed the cock of the city, in almost total disregard of the female, who had to spin, stalk, and saunter like a puppet following its master's moves.

In the bustling bar, European women sat drinking cocktails and watching the expertise of the locals. Terrino and I performed our own salsa style in a little corner away from the main dance area and enjoyed our brief performance. On the main stage, a couple of men were fighting their way through a complicated maze of moves. One, dressed in a white suite, *Grease* style, seemed to win the round with jerky ankle spirals. When they finished, the bar applauded. The men left their partners to search the crowd for new women with whom to show off their prowess. We watched from our table as the two men sloped through the congregation, trawling the floor for new bait. Suddenly, I broke out in a panic sweat. It was one of those moments when time froze. I kept repeating to myself, "Please no, not me, not me, I have blue feet, and I would be so embarrassed; besides, I am not dressed! Please, no!"

But the peacock in the white suit kept right on slinking in my direction. I turned my back and put my head down to drink my juice, hoping that I had mistaken his intention. My heart ticked too loud in the forever silence of the moment, knowing that I could not escape. A hand tapped my shoulder. I turned—it was him! He smiled endearingly, but I felt so intimidated, inadequate, unready to face the ordeal. Maria laughed. She knew how I felt!

I had never felt estranged from my legs and feet. I always knew that I could dance, yet in that moment, none of my limbs seemed attached to me. His touch was soft but firm, and he expected me to follow his intricate moves. I was awkward, too aware of my ugly blue feet, and with beautiful women watching, finely attired for the occasion, and I dressed in my travelling jeans with limp, damp hair!

For a few moments, I was transported back to when I first learnt to dance with my grandfather, who was a brilliant ball-room dancer. When I was three, he and I would clear the floor every Saturday night and perform his favourite samba in front of all the village people at the local hop. I was not aware that it was an unusual spectacle; it had always just seemed natural to me. One Saturday when I was six, I was taken to a grand dancehall in a big city for a ball with my grandmother, but my Mother had dressed me in an old pink woollen jumper, a shabby plaid skirt, grey kneesocks, and old brown shoes. My grandmother found it difficult to contain her disappointment at my appearance, as she had saved up for the occasion and it was to be a big moment in my little life.

"Don't you have a pretty dress?" she asked softly. I just shook my head. I didn't feel bad until I entered the grand hall, with its sparkling chandeliers, massive live band, and beautiful ladies in long, sweeping ballgowns. I realised then how silly I must have appeared to everyone, but my grandmother led me out onto the dance floor with pride, and I let the joy of the dance take over my shame. At that moment in Antigua, I could not let the joy of the dance take over. I felt a complete novice and wanted to crawl away into a corner.

I let him think I couldn't dance, and he softened to my awkwardness. My pride was dented as he slowed down all his moves to a snail's pace and even counted the timing out loud for me! The music seemed to go on forever, and I hated every moment. When the last cadence faded, he politely thanked me, and I rushed back to my seat to hide. Maria laughed and applauded, but I knew it was terrible. Just then, Miguel, our teacher, appeared and drew me off my seat. He expected me to put into practice all that I had learnt that evening. I couldn't let him or myself down; it was a second chance to redeem the Dance!

The fight came from within, and I drew up the energy and concentration to win the battle. We threw ourselves into the rhythm, twisting, turning, swaying as though we knew each other's moves intimately. Passion passed through both of our bodies, and an electric force encircled the circles we painted on the floor. This time, the music was over too soon and the thunder of applause distant. I was triumphant! My faith in myself was restored. Miguel had believed in me like my grandmother had in the magnificent ballroom!

Miguel then danced with Maria gently, coaxing her through the steps she had learnt earlier. I sat musing on how a dance partner is like a marriage. With the wrong person, all the moves are out of time, you feel awkward and unsure of the natural motion, which should flow eloquently between two people. I had had two failed marriages because I could not make the steps work when there was disharmony between us. With the right partner, the world could spin in a whirl of ecstasy. I was yet to find that person.

It was time to move on and leave the cocks crowing until the early hours. We stepped out into the electric night storm, which thrashed us with warm rain that beat our backs as we raced down the flooded streets. More rain, more wet shoes, more dye, more bluer-than-blue feet!

12

Brave Mountain Women and Their Story in the Swamp

Maria was fine in the night and did not suffer any ill consequences from eating her street snack. Everyone had gone on separate activities, and I was left sitting in the little turtle den. The lizard faces were motionless, ancient, in their shells, prehistoric cracked-backed creatures, unchanged forever. Inwardly for me, there was change. The journey had made me feel more alive and had helped to scrape away layers of complacency. Before the trip, I had become imprisoned in the humdrum treadmill of daily existence. As I watched the slow laborious, squat turtle heave its shell over the damp flagstones, every move torturous, I mused that as mundane routine stales a marriage, it also sucks out the life force, draining passion, until one day you wake up beside a stranger, not a husband.

I remembered when I learnt of my second husband's infidelity. I tried to attack him with a glass of wine, but it broke in my hand, splattering blood and wine, an unholy communion, across the sitting-room walls. Bits of glass lodged in the palm of my hand as I squeezed on the bitter truth. Sitting in the hospital, watching the doctor carefully pick out sharp shards, I felt alive in that moment, everything magnified. Alive: Living: Breathing: Being. As I watched the doctor gently stitch the jagged skin back together, I felt pain; pain meant life.

The harsh reality of this expedition has made me want to fight, has made me feel that something, someone, somewhere over the rainbow, there's a place for me, somewhere a space for me . . . I had been afraid to search for myself and find nothing! Find a dead cell of used electrodes with no energy to fuel the vibration of living. Life, death, birth, Earth's diurnal, eternal round, day-in, day-out, preparing for the last breath like the final brief flicker before the fire turns to ash.

When I was small, I could smell death; it was a sweet pungent odour that hung around its target. I always knew when someone was going to die because the person would exude that peculiar smell. I was about three years old, staying with my grandmother, which is where I spent most of my time, living in a row of small houses near the river, surrounded by fields and meadows. One sunny morning, I ambled down the back of the yards and walked into a house. I didn't know the elderly couple living there, but they knew me and smiled a warm welcome. Like many young children who don't have to have a reason for their actions, I had no idea why I was staring up at them in their neat kitchen. I was just there at that time. They made me very welcome and picked me up to sit on their sofa. They didn't have any children's books or toys, so they gave me a heavy catalogue to peruse and a drink of lemonade from a dusty glass, but as I sat there, the smell tore the air, permeated their words, hung around them, followed them like a bleak shadow. I couldn't drink the fusty liquid, and, pushing the cumbersome book off my lap, I slipped out into the bright sunshine without saying a word.

I didn't talk about my visit, but the next morning, there was a hushed commotion among the houses. Men in black suits with notepads stood asking the neighbours questions. I overheard a woman say to my grandmother," Yes, shocking, isn't it! They were found by the milkman, dead, both with their heads in the gas oven, lying side-by-side on the floor!"

The news was frightening. I had known that they were going to die because of the smell, but I hoped it wasn't me who had caused them to commit suicide. I didn't dare tell anyone about my visit. As I grew up, I lost the ability to know and smell the signs of death, yet I would know it instinctively again.

Life, birth, death, and the struggle for survival is heightened by the dire poverty of these people eking out a meagre existence, especially in the mountains surrounding Antigua, where the customs, traditions, and superstitions still hold the women captive. All except nine women in the village of Santiago Zamora, whose brave fight to improve their children's lives through medicine and education is beginning to be known and accepted. Being interested in their fight, I had arranged with Maria, Gunte, and three strangers from China to be picked up that afternoon to witness their achievements for ourselves. The three young Chinese girls arrived at our pensione to wait for a small, dirty white truck, which clanked its way down the uneven cobbles to transport us up into the mountains. A small Indian man beamed a wide smile as he bundled everyone into the open back, and I guess, as I was the oldest, he showed me into the front seat which was torn with no springs.

The drive through the city was a fairground experience, a bumper-car ride, a merry-go-round weaving in and out of traffic and a mini roller coaster as we began the ascent into the mountains. The broken seat was uncomfortable, but it was preferable to riding in the back without any at all! We passed through some small outlets nestled in the thick forest before arriving into Santiago Zamora village, where we were met by a handful of waving women. Romana seemed to be the leader, and, again because of my seniority, she came to my side and explained that it was too difficult and dangerous for the women to speak openly in the village, so we had to walk to a nearby swamp. It was thrilling to trek through coffee and banana plantations and see the crops growing, knowing that the next time back home, when I visited a supermarket to buy Guatemalan coffee, I would know the authenticity of the beans.

The afternoon rain had refreshed the trees, leaving gem droplets softly dripping off the branches as we brushed through the forest. The air was clear and moist, and also bracing from the dusty city below. The ground was damp and slippery in places as we followed the women in reverent silence. It was a clandestine meeting, an undercover arrangement with the rebellious nine women who had to sneak to the worst part of the forest to relate their secret plans. A man walked past bearing a huge, long bundle of wood on his shoulders, pretending that the women did not exist and that we visitors were invisible. He knew the women's intentions and chose to ignore our presence. Romana did not acknowledge him either and smiled as she asked me about my children and family; she was interested to learn about the Western woman's way of life. As we walked and talked together like old friends, sharing the bond of womanhood, even though my Spanish was weak, we communicated on a deeper level. Her soft, brown eyes, full of pain, pride, and wisdom, spoke more than her words. Our lifestyles, our cultures were so divergent, yet here, deep in the rain forest, I felt that I had found a sister.

After about fifteen minutes trek through the fertile forest, we came upon a plot that had been cleared and laid with a white concrete base. The women were proud of their basketball court, which they had built themselves with the money they raised from selling their handicrafts to visitors. The pitch sat incongruously, in the middle of the rain forest next to a swamp and surrounded in a fuzz of mosquitoes. It was a blatant, heart-breaking statement, a piece of architectural rebellion representing the women's determination to provide some modern facilities for their children. But the fact that it was built next to a swamp, like our meeting, meant that it was not wholly accepted.

Some of the women sat on the edge of the block base with their small children clutching at their skirts and peering at the strangers who were interested in their mothers' mutinous activities. I hoped for their sake that the court was used and appreciated, but a nagging doubt floated above the image of the brave nine women who stood victoriously before us, laying down an old plastic sheet in the middle of a swamp for us to sit on!

We sat in a veil of black insects and, to protect my face, I drew up the hood of my waterproof jacket, applying copious amounts of mosquito repellent, the expedition kind, that I had bought in York, which at that moment seemed like another life-time far removed from the swampland. Naquita stepped forward in her best long skirt and blouse, all hand-embroidered, to give her prepared speech about the women's battle against the traditions of their village. I have attended many lectures in various venues, but never one so strange as a mosquito-swamp battle-ground, straining to listen to the talk through a low, constant, orchestral insect symphony!

Like a schoolgirl giving her first class talk, Naquita stood with her hands laid over her pretty apron, her sleek black hair tied in a bun at the nape of her neck, her wide Indian features, weather-worn from her harsh life and childbearing, becoming girlish when she smiled. She explained that the small group of women were in their tenth year of the project and that it had been a hard struggle but well worth the ordeal. The traditions of their people were so ingrained in the fabric of their daily life that it was difficult to break away. The men of the village did not want their women to be emancipated in any way, and they certainly did not want their children to be educated. The women had formed a cooperative through which they sold their handiwork to visitors to save enough money to buy materials for a school. They had foreign help in the building and had made enough money to employ one teacher for a short while each year. Many older women in the village deliberately made their lives difficult, but they wanted to be part of the modern world and not have so many children. When the idea of contraception was brought into the village, many young women were punished for taking the Pill, and still within families there was strong resistance to change, but the circle of nine women remained adamant and were even beginning to influence others.

At the end of the talk, we applauded the women, momen-tarily forging a clearing through the black mist of insects as we beat the air with our hands. Romana came to my side and explained we were going to walk a short way to see the small surgery they had built. After the talk, we were more aware of being watched from afar and suspiciously viewed the empty village as we ambled through the main square. A dog ran out, barking his displeasure at our presence, but was hastily retrieved by a child, who dragged him back indoors. There was a distinct air of unwelcoming tolerance in the empty streets, but behind the curious shutters, another world existed.

We stopped outside a small concrete outhouse, which was the newly built surgery. The green wooden door (which resembled the one to my grandmother's coalhouse) was unlocked with pride as we were shown inside. There was a table, two chairs. and a few cupboards full of pills, bandages, potions, lotions, and needles.

"We have a Norwegian doctor who visits us once a week", explained Anita. I asked her what happened if someone became sick when the doctor wasn't around. Anita shrugged her shoulders and said, "If it is a child, one of the men runs down the mountain and stops a chicken bus. He has to persuade the driver to motor all the way up the mountain with his passengers to take the sick one to the nearest hospital."

"And if it is a grown-up?" I enquired.

"It is not quite the same; we wait!"

Further on, a young woman lingered, holding a tiny baby boy, whose name was Rodrigo. I loved him immediately, and she allowed me to hold and cuddle him. He didn't cry but looked at me with laughing eyes. I carried him a short way to a cluster of huts, where I handed him back to his loving mother. We entered a compound of huts made of slats of wood and old sheets of plastic with adobe walls. The floor was bare, black earth with a few reed mats in places. It was dark inside, with splinters of light cutting through the cracks in between the wooden poles. It was hard to believe this was their home and not a makeshift play den. The women had set out their handicrafts in the style of a shop, with their wares neatly placed on trestle tables, each piece of work labelled with the maker's name and clearly priced. Above the tables was a huge sign they had written in English using a child's markers on shiny white paper:

WELCOME TO SANTIAGO ZAMORA AND OUR TOUR

It was evident that they had made extensive preparations for our visit and that they wanted to please us. A small arena was set in the middle of the hut, made out of assorted chairs and stools, where we all sat like a circus crowd waiting for the show to begin. Romana began initially by laying long strands of reeds in front of us, magically twisting them into shape, making a mat swiftly and easily. She appreciated our "oohs" and "ahs" and smiled with an embarrassed glance at me. Two of the other women deftly used the same technique to make a fan and a floor mat. Then two other women gave us a weaving demonstration, which was fascinating, as they threw the shuttle back and forth with speed and alacrity to create dazzling patterns in myriad bright colours, as in everything they wore.

In many of the villages, part of the staple diet is black tortillas, and a large woman brought in the maize to grind on an old, black block of rock, where she ground it into a powdery flour with a stone roller. Three other women sat by the open fire ready to knead it into dough and shape it into round pancakes to heat over the crackling fire. Next, Romana showed us some multicoloured pebbles in a coconut husk. She explained that they were freshly picked coffee beans, and she rolled them out on the same black block, removing the initial husks, which she passed around for us to examine. The coffee beans were not what I had seen in the shops back home, and I was amazed to discover the different hues of colours on the outer shells. Then Romana crushed the beans on the block and collected the stubble into a pot, over which she poured boiling water from an old black kettle.

"This is coffee," she proclaimed, pouring some of the liquid into an old mug for me to sample. Warily I allowed a little to pass my lips, pretending to drink it enthusiastically. I was disappointed with the flavour, which didn't taste like coffee at all but a strange, sour elixir. Not wishing to upset her, I disposed of the contents into the bare earth when no one was looking.

Black tortillas, freshly cooked over the open fire, were passed around. I only broke off a small segment to eat, as, like before, they felt and tasted like cardboard. Chickens running around inside the entrance to the compound clucked and squawked occasionally until they met their timely death and were served up in a watery stew, which I only picked at, not wishing to aggravate my stomach condition. A baby girl sat on her mother's knee watching us, eating the same stew, which she lapped up voraciously, making me feel guilty for not tucking into my portion with the same enthusiasm.

At the end of the meal, the women collected money from us for the tour and the food inviting us to look at the goods for sale. I wanted to buy something that Romana had made and picked up a small purse which she had woven. I found her alone in another chamber clearing up the plates, washing them in an old bucket of cold water. The rain began again, splashing through a hole in the tin roof creating a black muddy patch next to a stone step overgrown with green slime and moss. I gave Romana money for her purse and extra to help her. She stood up, shyly wiping her hand on her bright apron. She was smaller than I, and, staring up into my eyes from my shoulders, she reached up to my forehead and placed her index finger into the spot between my eyebrows. I knew what she was doing. Ceremoniously, I did the same to her and we exchanged an unspoken moment of truth.

The past came spinning back into my mind and out again like a spark, igniting incidents into a spurious fusion of understanding . . .

I remembered the morning when my mother announced at breakfast, "She sleeps with her eyes open," referring to me in a quasi-mocking tone.

"Don't you know you sleep with your eyes wide open?" she questioned coldly.

I was only six years old and found her outburst, another layer of blame, something else I did wrong which displeased her. As a small child of three she had taken me to the doctor, complaining that I was mentally disturbed because I spoke to invisible people for hours on end. She was adamant that it wasn't just a child's imaginary response to a play situation; she was convinced that it was something deep and ugly. The doctor said that I had a rich imagination and I would soon grow out of it.

I had forgotten the incident until many years later, when, stuck in an unhappy marriage, my husband began a quarrel in bed, threatening me physically. Suddenly an eye appeared in the middle of my forehead, so terrifying him that he shot out of the room. The marriage was over from that moment on, and to this day he can recall the sight of the eye staring at him, even relating the event to our daughters. In the horror of reckoning, my mother's words flew back, hanging in the gloomy air, darkly foreboding above the bed as it dawned upon me what she had seen all those years previously—a third eye!

Similarly, I was with an artist friend on a long night vigil to keep watch on a house, but I fell asleep rolled up in the dark on the carpet. In his words he explained that he was sitting nearby with his knees curled up into his chest. He had glanced over at me and became fascinated by a strange blue light that danced across my face. He tried to trace the source, but in the bleak night, there was no light, not even a street lamp. He became engrossed in the blue translucent beam and saw that I wasn't asleep but had my eyes open. He moved closer but was astonished to see I was asleep with my eyes closed, except there was an eye in the middle of my forehead staring at him. Overcoming his shock, and being an artist, he took out his torch, notebook, and pencil and sketched what he saw. He produced a lovely picture for me from the experience and later was witness to many strange and unbelievable events.

The idea of the "third eye" in its mythical basis is acceptable in many cultures, even affording safety from evil if hung above doors and windows; in its iconic form, it is a sea of blues on a white background, but the deeper knowledge of knowing that other people have seen it in reality is hard to accept. There in the moment of an unprompted ritual with Romana, though, it was natural and spontaneous as we honoured the sign of ancient knowledge by touching each other's foreheads, releasing coiled energy into the Universe; pure tokens of force between priestesses, watched by the eyes from another world, our eyes, our third eye deep in the rain forest, high up in the mountain village of Santiago Zamora.

13

Flores: Bending Time

The drive back to the pensione was just as uncomfortable as the ride to Santiago Zamora, but it didn't seem to take so long. I kept my sadness at leaving Romana in my heart and smiled at the little man driving, making polite conversation, until we clanked and hobbled back to our guesthouse. The Chinese girls drifted away into the evening as Maria and I returned to our room. There, we packed our gear in readiness for the early-morning start to catch a small army aircraft to Flores, a tiny island by Lake Peten Itza.

Before our last evening meal in Antigua, Terrino called a meeting in the library to discuss the plans for the next day. We all needed to pay him for the flight. As I handed over my money, I glanced briefly at Gordon and smiled a secret thanks. There was paperwork to organise and permits for travelling, permits for crossing over borders, and permits to leave the country. It took a while for everyone to produce passports, health documents, and special grants to visit countries from various embassies, before Terrino could inform us about the next part of the journey. We would have to leave the pensione at three in the morning.

Punctuality was vital. The army aircraft would not wait for any late arrivals. We were travelling north, past Rio Dulce and Poptun to Flores, an idyllic tiny island set next to a tropical lake. Formerly, Flores was the city of Tayasal, founded by the

Spanish in 1700. It had been an island until recent years, when a causeway was built to connect it to the mainland; until then it had grown most of its own crops and sold chicle farmed from trees to be used in the manufacture of gum.

Terrino explained that many of the local people on the island still used their own unique style of canoe, a cayuco, which is a small, dug-out boat hewn from one long piece of wood. He said that the island was very small and that one could walk around its front street and back street within a short time. The streets were ancient cobbles with uneven surfaces, so we would have to be careful. The houses, unique to the area with brightly painted facades and thatched roofs, added to the charm of the island. We were to spend two nights there, so we would have ample time to explore the place, buy local handicrafts, enjoy the hotel set by the lake edge, and even swim in the lake, or go fishing, canoeing, bird watching, or visit the tiny nature reserve or the small zoo.

The Complainers were friendly and relaxed after spending a day by themselves sightseeing and were looking forward to the next stage of the journey. Everyone decided to eat together, and I suggested an extraordinary bijou place I had found that was owned by a gay French artist. The café/restaurant was furnished like a sitting room but with everything outside, in a luscious jungle courtyard—even the bathroom was outdoors! It was a crazy, topsy-turvy world least expected in an ordinary setting.

I found the place purely by chance wandering down a side street. The smell of fresh coffee percolating through the bright morning seduced me to slip through a mysterious, battered, high-fenced gate into a magical sphere, isolated from the compressed flat houses and squalid drains. No one was around, only the coffee bubbled, the glass catching the first rays of sun glinting through the bird of paradise flowers perforated with morning dew. I called out, but no one appeared, so I meandered through the exciting paintings, sculptures, and pieces of art displayed like a private collection in someone's home. I felt like an interloper, voyeuristically enjoying a secret feast. Suddenly, a voice behind me asked, "Can I 'elp you?"

A small man with a goatee smiled. I told him that I admired his paintings. He preened like a forest peacock and gave me a private viewing of all his work. Anton was a gifted artist, and I was thrilled by the whole café, set out like a 1930s French gaiety theatre. The coffee was the best I had tasted on the entire journey, and he daintily arranged chocolate coffee beans on a side plate as an accompaniment. To my surprise, the raw coffee beans wrapped in solid chocolate seemed to soothe my stomach, giving me an inner feeling of contentment and healing, which I hadn't previously felt during the entire journey. When I left, I asked where to buy them. He smiled wistfully and I promised to return with friends.

Standing outside the high wooden wall that evening, there was no sign of life. It was as though the place had been abandoned for centuries, with a forest overgrowth on the walls, like Sleeping Beauty's after the wicked witch's curse. Old signs of menus hung precariously from a sidewall, faintly painted and erased in places. There were no light inside the building. I was disappointed, saddened—there had to be someone there! I rattled the chains in desperation. The others looked at me strangely.

"Come on, let's find somewhere else," urged Gordon, turning me away. We all agreed and tramped back down the street to the main square. I felt thwarted in my quest to show the others the unusual café and frustrated not to have kept my promise to Anton, but somehow, perhaps I knew I never would, for he was part of another world, lost in the past which I had accidentally stumbled upon!

Maria's high-pitched alarm woke us at two-thirty the next morning. We scrambled out of bed and dressed in the cool of the dark. We packed our belongings and closed the door for the last time on our convent retreat. The turtles, statuesque in the gloom, slept in the jungle garden. Yawning, we boarded a small bus and bounced along the uneven, potholed streets of a sleepy Antigua. No one spoke and, before long, we were unpacking our rucksacks and trundling into the army airport office. A few sleepy soldiers waited in the small lounge, but I was surprised to see quite a few civilians making use of the army post and packages flight.

As dawn streaked the sky with firefly flashes of pink, we were escorted to the small waiting aircraft. All procedures were met with precision, and we soon took off into the new day. We were served biscuits and a handful of sweets, together with a soft drink, but I didn't eat anything, as my stomach was churning again. The flight took under an hour and, before long, we were alighting into the bright sunshine of a different world.

We arrived at our hotel before nine o'clock and as we dumped our rucksacks from the small bus into the lobby, we were met by efficient waiters. It was the first time on the whole of the journey that I felt we were in a clean, decent hotel. Maria and I were shown to our room on the top floor. It was fine, but I spied a small gecko in the corner next to my bed and involuntarily I shuddered. I told myself not to react and try to enjoy the new place. The bathroom was up a few steps and, on opening the window, I gazed at an amazing view. The skyline was a conglomeration of dilapidated red tin roofs and medieval thatched ones standing on concrete stalks about three or four stories high with myriad telegraph poles and electric cables crossing and criss-crossing the town, which was surrounded by an azure lake and, in the distance, lush, green mountains.

I washed my underwear and jeans and hung them out to dry over the open window, viewing families in apartments opposite immersed in their daily routines. I was lucky in that moment not to have any semblance of a daily routine, only travel, survive, travel, endure, travel, enjoy, travel and soak up each experience to savour and recall at a later date.

It was wonderful to be a regular tourist for a couple of days, with a chance to sunbathe by a modest pool overlooking the enticing tropical lake. Our party slumped into the luxurious chairs by the pool, enjoying cool beers and cocktails, while a couple of smart businessmen completed their breakfast meeting, shaking hands as they walked through a huddle of half-dressed Europeans. Swimsuits and bikinis were sported for the first time among our party, and it was good to see everyone shaking off the journey stress. Sore toes and swollen ankles and knees were bathed in the open and displayed by the pool as jokes about each other were bandied playfully across the parapet. From our vantage point, we could see a few locals swimming in the lake and a family returning from shopping in their cayuko. Life seemed slow, peaceful, and calm, almost ordinary, as Gordon ordered more cool beers in rising heat. Ella, Maria, and I decided to take a stroll along the lake edge at lunchtime.

Just beneath the hotel a few yards away, families lived in poor apartments, but the slow pace of life in the heat and magnificence of the lake gave their poverty a rare dignity. They coped with their lot and made the most of what they had. Walking in the heat was unbearable, so we stopped at the nearest restaurant, situated on the lake itself. We sat under a bright red canopy set against the turquoise lake under a baby blue sky puffed with white doughnut clouds and ordered a range of dishes, which smelt wholesome and aromatic. It was a girl's lunch, a real treat, so civilised after the rough passage through different countries. It was as though we were old friends, meeting *Sex in the City* style, for a light bite to eat while discussing clothes, men, and the cost of living. We spent a couple of hours lazily enjoying our lunch on the lake. It was wonderful not to have to worry about schedules or race to catch the next bus. It was sheer bliss just to relax.

Maria and I ambled around the town after our filling meal. She needed to reimburse her purse and had an endless supply of money from her parents. I needed to track down some good batteries for my camera, having been duped in most countries into buying half-used ones! We both found what we needed and enjoyed browsing the shops. I lusted after a new pair of white trousers displayed in a shop window but was disappointed not to find the right size. Immediately a curious lady came out from behind a pile of multicoloured T-shirts, assuring me that her sister could make me a pair of linen trousers in my size in just under an hour! I agreed to the transaction and arranged to go back to the shop later.

The heat was intense, so we strolled back to the shade of the hotel, where we relaxed under the cool of the palms and let the afternoon drift obliviously away. As promised, my trousers were ready and were beautifully made in the right size. The price was cheap, and I was grateful to have something nice to wear for dinner, as everyone had arranged to meet in a special restaurant that Terrino had said was the best on the island. In my dressy top and new trousers, I wandered down to the lakeside just as the brilliant orange sun was setting, washing the sky radiantly with gold, purples, and pinks. It was a perfect picture, but for me, there was one element missing: someone to share it!

Just at that moment, I saw a young girl standing by a broken tree, its old branches trailing aimlessly into the lapping waves. She stood waiting, occasionally glancing from side to side, her young, beautiful face caught in expectancy and delightful anticipation. A rustle through some nearby bushes caught her attention as a young man carrying his jacket nonchalantly over his shoulder appeared and snatched her to his chest greedily. I was embarrassed to spy on their hungry love and turned away to walk against the fading sun, stupidly allowing a song to drift into my head. Unfortunately, earning a living from choreographing well-known musicals, I am often plagued at inopportune moments by appropriate songs which spring to mind . . .

Hello, young lovers, wherever you are . . . I had a love of my own like yours, I had a love of my own!

Unfortunately, it was too apt, catching me off-guard as the melody struck a minor chord of self-pity. I turned to take a last glimpse at the happy couple, but the sky had turned black against an inky blue lake dotted with diamond flecks. The passion of the moment, like the sun, had slipped away. The Blue Moon Restaurant, with its high ceiling, multicultural décor, and long wooden tables was inviting and charismatic, with bold original paintings and beautiful wall hangings blending into the dark-blue walls. It was run by a friendly European couple, who were proud of their successful venture and made us feel at home, producing red wine in large, earthen pots. The menu was adventurous, tempting us with exotic dishes. The wine was excellent and soothing after the heat of the lazy day, releasing the fun sprite amongst us, allowing a brief, "holiday" pause in our continuous struggle to keep up. We stayed the whole night and rolled back to the hotel before midnight. I hadn't forgotten the gecko and tried to establish its whereabouts before pulling the sheet over my head. It wasn't in the corner. My head reeled with its possible location, but the wine and the lovely evening lulled me into a satisfying slumber.

The next morning was also civilised. The hotel had a restaurant where we could breakfast. That was a luxury we hadn't expected. Normally, we had to search for somewhere to eat. I ordered poached eggs and waited as the others slowly drifted in. They were relaxed, building up to the next challenge, which was our trek through the rain forest jungle at the dead of night, to climb to the highest temple in Tikal, Temple IV.

Now the others have gone to explore the island, but I want to rest. I am in the shade watching the clear lake, where time is a gentle breeze wafting across my face. Time is, was, and perhaps, will be tomorrow, but now is all I know, where the "I" is suspended above the water, hovering, rippling, riding the gentle waves. Mingling, watching, being with others who have yet no earthly form, waiting for their turn to slip into time and ride the curve of nurture; dipping into the warmth of succour, as the red sun beats; ticking forever in the never-before moment where caverns, cages of white bones, form like coral in the womb of all oceans.

Who are these beings? I do not know, I cannot say, they have always existed.

Do they have voices?

Yes.

"Do you want anything, please?"

A waiter hovers over my shoulder, and I lift my sunglasses to reply.

"Er, no, thank you!"

I return from my thoughts back to the sunshine, where time has slipped to midday. I am hungry. I order a salad, which I eat while watching the birds glide over the lake. I am grateful to have this moment. I am grateful to have danced my Songline. I am grateful to have been under the spotlight, out in the fray, under the moonbeams, and now, far, far away from my worries. I must not let the thought of the tax investigator ruin my peace, but momentarily, the nightmare taunts me, haunts me. What if I am stripped of all I have? I battle to turn over the thought, slide it down a mountain of doubt and bury it in the quicksand below. I am distracted by a little bird hopping near my side and am amazed to note it only has one leg. It makes such a brave attempt to hide its disability. I hold my breath as it comes close enough for me to see into its eyes. It stops. It returns my gaze. My heart thumps too loud as I remain deathly still. I do not want to frighten it. Little bird, what do you want to say to me? Its unearthly stare, glaring at me with his head on one side as though it is wondering how to tell me I am a foolish creature. It stays, almost admonishing me, for a few minutes longer, then hops backward a few steps before turning to fly into the breeze to glide away with ease across the lake.

The bird's appearance jolts my memory to two extraordinary, timeless brushes with nature. The first when I was nineteen years old staying in Coonoor, in the Nilgiris in south India. I had an errand in the next village, Ooticamund, to collect some herb cheese made by an English lady who lived near the library. It was early morning, and the cool mountain mist swirled thickly around the church as I made my way over to the library. The veil was so dense, I couldn't see anything. Suddenly, through the vapour, a head appeared. Stealthily, a creature crept through the fog, its striking features bathed in the warmth of its hot breath. I froze. The tiger chose not to see me, and passed, keeping low to the ground. I almost called out in fear and delight as three little cubs followed her through the white haze. They didn't make a sound. They were beautiful. The memory fills me with awe.

The second was years later, when I was driving home to Yorkshire from London, where I was choreographing a show. I had to drive through the night in order to teach early the next morning. Turning into the road leading to the rural village where Richard the Third built his castle, the light was just lifting from grey to blue over the ancient ruins, and the dawn chorus echoing through the meadows. I slowed down, opening the window to breathe in the cool, clean air after the dirt and grime of London. Suddenly, a sharp movement to my side made me stop. A beautiful fawn stood beside my car; he was so close that I could reach out and stroke his nose. I gazed into his deep brown, innocent eyes. He was Walt Disney's Bambi, with long, black eyelashes and gangly legs. I treasured that moment. It was enchanting, surreal, lasting only seconds, for just as quickly as he had bounced over the hedge, he leapt back, leaving me wondering if it had really happened.

Voices brought me back to the lakeside. Ella and Gordon had visited the butterfly garden and were delighted by all the different species on display.

"What kind of a morning have you had, then?"

"Oh, I've done nothing really, needed to rest!" I replied casually, switching off my meditation mode.

Ella was excited about our next venture into the jungle, talking about what she had read about Tikal.

"It says here," said Ella informatively, showing me the guidebook, "that UNESCO states that Tikal is the 'Heritage of Humanity'. What do you suppose that means?" She leaned over my lounge chair showing me the amazing view from Temple IV, which we were going to climb and watch the dawn rise over the rain forest.

"I think it means it's probably the best, the biggest, and the most mysterious of all the Mayan remains," I replied, not really knowing the answer.

She continued reading. "It says the Mayans were obsessed with the idea of time!"

I didn't hear the rest of the sentence, as the phrase had hit a nerve. Perhaps I am obsessed by what time *isn't*, having always slipped in and out of it unexpectedly. My problem was knowing what is real and what is imagination and whether imagination is more "real" than life. I know I have the ability to bend time, but only in dire circumstances and usually when my children are involved, like the time when my youngest daughter had gone to the cinema with a friend and her mother. I promised to meet them outside the cinema at seven o'clock. It was a Saturday

107

evening, and I was watching television with my son. We had become engrossed in a documentary, when I noticed it was five minutes to seven. I panicked. I lived twenty two miles away from town, down tiny country lanes with a motorway to negotiate, plus Saturday night traffic in the town centre. I was never going to make it! My daughter would be distraught to think I had forgotten her, as she was only six and having a fretful time during my divorce period.

I took a deep breath and closed my eyes for a few seconds. My son understood what I was doing. I had to push myself into a trance state. I found a deep vibration out beyond the universe, where time hangs in a void like a taut wire pulled by the Earth. I leant my being on it as though I were lying on a tightrope at the top of a circus tent and slowed down the minutes, the seconds, the microseconds, with my energy. Then got in my car, focusing and concentrating on impeding the normal time zone only for the ones involved in the operation.

As I hurried, my actions outside my body were speedy, but inside my head it was macro-slow. I had left the house at nearly seven o'clock, and the film finished at seven, so it was amazing that I pulled up outside the cinema just as they were walking out! I felt elated, relieved, and so glad to see her little face break out in a huge beam as she clambered into the car, full of the fun of her excursion. On returning home my son was not in the least surprised that I had fulfilled my mission.

Back by the lakeside, Gordon brought us both drinks and sat back in the cool of the shade listening to Ella continue her expose on Tikal. "Tikal is said to be the most spiritually empowered spot on Earth! The City of the Dead, the seat of the great Jaguar lords, and the place where the Maya created the concept of 'zero' in their number system." She paused, sipping her drink slowly, "It's the grandest city in the history of the world!"

"That's certainly something, then," laughed Gordon, finishing his beer.

They stayed for a while chatting about our instructions from Terrino, how we had to cover up from head to toe in the jungle to protect ourselves from insects, leeches, mosquitoes, and snakes. Tikal was only half an hour's drive away, and it was going to be a great adventure trekking through the rain forest in the dead of night. It was going to be a challenge, but I had no idea just how tricky it was going to be for me.

Neither did I know that having wished for a romantic liaison, it would come true in the most unexpected and unwarranted way!

14

Tikal: Dance with Danger

Where is the now?
Dark, night, with only the moon watching.

It is early March. Cutting, bitter winter winds screech around my conservatory.

The tax investigation is under way, and I am afraid. I comply with the wishes of a very officious woman, but still she digs and digs. I am being victimised and write a letter accusing her of this. She is dragging out the investigation and will have a share of the final figure. I kept back some money to send my son to university. I was struggling alone; I never took anything for myself or ever demanded anything from the government; I always worked and paid my own way. I know it was wrong, but I had no other option and I would do the same again. I am not sorry and I am not contrite. But I am fearful of what is going to happen to me.

I sit wrapped in my coat watching my friend the moon, remembering a different kind of fear . . . fear in the jungle!

There was no point in going to bed that night, when we were all to meet just after midnight outside our hotel in Flores to drive to Tikal National Park, where a special guide would escort us through the jungle. Our aim was to climb Temple IV before dawn to experience the magic of Tikal as the first rays of sunlight hit the forest. We were all dressed for the trek, but as we tumbled along the cobbled streets, Terrino realised that

110

he had forgotten to ask us to bring torches, so between seven of us, there were only two! In the safety of the bus, it didn't seem such a big deal, as everyone was fired up for the adventure, not realising what was in store.

The short drive through the Central Peten Peninsula from Flores to Tikal was uneventful, as it was dark and there was nothing to see. As we climbed out of the bus, the jungle acoustics electrified the night with unrecognisable sounds from every direction, like the fine tuning of instruments before a concert. Our guide was soft-spoken and had the gentle gait of a benign giant. Light from the warden's hut broke the dark, and shadows from the bushes darted behind us. But as we began making our way through the thick vegetation, the night closed in. Bleak, dense black blinded me, shutting out my light like a coffin lid. I couldn't see anything.

I can't breathe in the dark! I can't move! I can't see! I am being left behind! I can't . . .

I reached out to young Gunte, who had a torch. I clutched his waterproof jacket and clung on leechlike. I was shaking with fear. He could feel my terror and, although I was a hindrance to his every move, he tolerated me. He shone the torch on the ground so that I could see where I was walking, but in front of me, there was sheer blackness. I could only feel my way forward by holding onto Gunte's jacket while keeping my eyes on the ground. But rising panic boiled up from my legs, through my stomach, and into my chest. I couldn't take in air. I was dizzy.

Stop! Please, stop! I can't go on! I can't see! I can't breathe . . .

The jungle path was becoming steeper, and I found it hard on my injured knee. The slippery earth, wet from the afternoon rains, made the going tough. I had borrowed a pair of socks from Maria to wear with my blue sandals, but they were not the ideal footwear for the forest bed.

Trekking up further, I was hot, cocooned inside my waterproof gear from head to toe. My panic simmered, almost reaching a boiling point as pain seared inside my chest. I couldn't go on!

Help, please, someone! I am lost, lost inside myself, I can't see! I can't breathe . . .

111

Wet leaves brushed my nose. A howl growled and gurgled next to my face on my right. I felt the creature's breath on my eyelids. The howler monkey was so close, so near. What did it look like? I had never seen or heard one before. Another yowl wailed a reply to my left.

Pain! Pain! In my chest. I can't breathe . . .

The howler, close to me, shrieked again, forcing monster images to leap out the crevices of my imagination to terrorise me.

Please, someone? My heart was coming up into my throat, breaking through my ribs . . .

The battle was inside. No one knew my distress except Gunte, who only felt part of my fear as I clutched his coat in desperation. No one else was afraid. The incline grew steeper. The blackness never became lighter; my eyes never became accustomed to the total blackout. The forest was an amphitheatre of invisible throbbing, clicking, squawking, squelching, growling, roaring messages from one monkey to another, mockingly warning of our approach.

No one else wanted to stop. No one showed signs of fear. I thought of my children and the children in my dance school. I had always taught them to carry on no matter what; I couldn't let them down. I needed to go deep into myself away from the reality and slow down my pulse, even out my heartbeat and try to breathe. Through each step, I forced myself to find a calm place within. I had learnt this lesson when I was twelve . . .

He was a young man, the youngest deputy head in the county. I was alone, having been given permission to complete a piece of sewing at lunchtime. There was a small corridor between the needlework and the art rooms. I was looking for a thread when he came through the opposite door.

"Ah, what are you doing here, little miss?"

"Nothing sir, just sewing. Mrs. Green said I could."

"Did she, now?

"Yes, sir."

"We'll see about that!"

He towered above me. I could smell his sweat. His short black hair fringed forward over his forehead as he peered down.

His black eyes showed no mercy. His thick glasses shaded his delight as he took my arm. I didn't resist, he was a teacher. I didn't understand! He slid his thumb and forefinger up my left arm and felt for the soft flesh below my armpit, glaring into my face, peering down so close that I could smell his rancid breath.

Then it began. The pain, the pinching the squeezing. I did not call out. I did not cry. I knew instinctively that if I did, his pleasure would be satisfied. Intuitively I found a quiet corner in my mind and hid there away from the physical torment. A sound in the classroom next door saved me from fainting. He moved on, disgruntled. I hid in the cupboard under the clothes rail, holding my arm. I tore the world to pieces with my silent sobs. My arm was a mess. He had burst the blood vessels. I was afraid to tell anyone.

As I reran the scene in my mind, I watched the lonely child and wished I could have comforted her. The memory had taken me onward, and the terrain had evened out. I realised that my breathing was better and my heart steadier. The howler monkeys were further away, and the thick brush had merged into forest. When we stopped for a while to catch our breath, I apologised to Gunte, who was too polite to complain. He became my guide through the dense forest bed. Without warning from under the opaque canopy, we emerged into a clearing, where the great temple loomed before us, swathed in a silver sheen, lighting a gossamer stairway to heaven!

I looked up at the scanty scaffolding, which had platforms in places. Nevertheless, the sheer steepness of the climb was daunting. At least I could see the steps. Poor Gunte was glad to be rid of me. I could tackle the climb, although my knee was not good. Up and up we ascended, sometimes pausing on a brief landing and then scaling onward tugging onto the side ropes. The climb was scary, but the last section to the very top was the worst, consisting of a vertical iron ladder with no rails! I didn't look down but kept my focus on the top ledge. Such a public access and no real safety holds! There was nothing to prevent anyone from falling straight over the crumbling edge into the forest below. I had to stretch my small legs up to the last foothold and was shocked to see a silent congregation meekly waiting for the roof of the world to break into a new beginning. I was afraid to step near the edge, as the crumbling rock fragmented beneath my uncertain foothold.

I edged my way through the hallowed gathering. It was like a Christmas midnight mass with unspoken rejoicing, everyone poised for that special, magical moment. A chill breeze blew across my hot, sweaty back. I shivered as I found a small ledge to perch on. This was it! This was the moment in time when the few who gathered would join the past with the present: together with priests and people of the lost Maya who had stood on the very same spot watching, waiting for the crack of dawn to flood the jungle, illuminating the temples.

In the nervous silence, I listened to the breath of the jungle. It inhaled and exhaled in time to the rhythm of the sea. It was the sigh of the sea. It was a mother's breast, undulating softly. Understanding came swiftly. In the silent second, I knew how the earth and water vibrated harmoniously into one living planet, becoming the resonance of all we see, hear, and know. Time held its breath before the sky splintered like the first tentative cracks of a duckling breaking out of its shell. The fractured sky wasn't pink or yellow or white, it was electric blue, flooding across the pea-green jungle. The blueness hung over the forest until a heavy grey uniformly washed above the trees as the birdsong broke the night spell.

I turned around and could see everyone clearly. The dim, shadowy figures of the night stood out boldly against the ancient bricks, which were gradually wearing away. There were people from different parts of the world; as strangers in the night, we had perched high on a pinnacle above the jungle spending an unforgettable, wondrous occasion together in secret union; not individuals, but one body watching each with our own thoughts. But then in the early morning light, we became strangers again, and it was time for everyone to start the day. Our group waited while others moved cautiously back down the ladder. I noticed the leader of a group who almost bounced past me wearing a striped, knitted tea-cosy hat. He was small, good-looking, and agile as a mountain goat, with a friendly smile.

When the coast was clear, we began the descent. My legs quivered with fear and muscle tension, but it wasn't as bad as the climb in the dark. We had taken a few biscuits to munch at the top and were to be given the chance to buy drinks and snacks later. The trees and the forest were a delight in the morning freshness, making me ashamed of my night terror. We found an ancient altar that had a tree stump growing out of its middle with myriad tiny insects scurrying all over it. It was a sad remnant from the past, a lonesome piece of evidence that civilisation had occupied that tiny space but had deserted, and the hungry jungle was quick to eat up the proof of the living, hiding the history of a lost people.

Maria stood by a tree whose girth would have housed at least ten people. She posed, and I took a photograph of her trying to hug the bark, enthralled by the size of the tree, having seen documentaries about such magnificent species. Toucans and macaws flashed their bright plumage through the mottled canopy above. Just as I was trying to follow a toucan to take a photograph, the handsome guide came running past. He stopped and looked at me.

"Here, let me do it!" he laughed as he took the camera from my hands.

I had no option but to follow, running to keep up with him. He took a couple of shots, which didn't turn out too well, but I thanked him nonetheless. He asked my name and said his was Alberto, that he was a guide and a taxi driver. He gave me his card and informed me that everyone took a break by the main temple at eleven where there was a vendor who sold drinks and snacks. He asked me to meet him there.

I was flattered by his unexpected attention. His dark eyes looking deeply into mine made me shiver. He made me feel feminine even though I had not slept, washed, or brushed my hair! There was a chemistry between us. I agreed to meet him. He ran back to his group, and I felt excited about the prospect of seeing him again. The world seemed different after our brief encounter. I felt a lightness of being. A girlish, rosy-warm glow inside permeated my thoughts. I laughed at myself. In the middle of a rain forest I had had a chance meeting with an interesting man who liked me! After my last failed relationship, I had lost all confidence in myself. I thought I was not desirable to anyone and would never fall in love again. Yet in Tikal, a magical, mysterious place, a man was attracted to me and I to him.

Wandering through the great antediluvian ruins, the sun was breaking through the dense cloud, highlighting the dewy foliage with bright gems. The air was clear and fresh with an earthy fragrance, unchanged since time itself. I clambered among the ancient, enigmatic boulders. Where did they come from, how did they get here? The same unanswered riddle has puzzled generations. Yet for me, I believe beings beyond our imagination were sent to help us. I feel their energy, know their wisdom, see their stamp everywhere. They have left their secrets in our blood, in the macrocosm of our intestines; already scientists have found the snake code hidden in our DNA, the double helix representing the snake god symbol, but they have yet to fathom the arcane message.

I scrambled over a small wall and stood in a corner overlooking the main parade of temples, finding a small stone to sit on to view the grandeur of the masonry. I wasn't sure whether the tingling vibration was the result of being in tune with the energy of the moment or my rising anticipation of seeing Alberto. I wished I could have had the chance to freshen up, but it wasn't possible. I closed my eyes and breathed in the pure air. I was so tired. I relaxed and drifted into a dream. I was floating down a long, winding tunnel under one of the temples, following a procession lead by Alberto dressed in Maya ceremonial attire, with a huge plumed headdress. It was dark, and the high-sided walls momentarily flared red from the goat's grease torches carried by menservants. Priests dressed in white and gold graciously held small boxes in their outstretched hands. Other servants carried distinctive gem-encrusted goblets on gold trays. When the party came to a halt, prayers were offered by a senior priest, who opened one of the boxes and withdrew what looked like small, brown beans. These he handed to a servant, who crushed them on a nearby sacrificial stone. The granules were collected and placed in a golden jug. Another servant poured a pail of steaming water over the infusion, releasing a familiar smell of rich, dark chocolate. Other ingredients were ritualistically added to the chant of prayers. Ripe plum chilies, spices, and a thick red liquid were stirred, and the resulting brew was poured into the ornate goblets, which were handed out to the five guests of honour. The men slowly sipped the beverage with careful pleasure. I guessed that the brew was a healing, empowering potion. I remembered how I felt after tasting the chocolate coffee beans in Antigua and how they soothed my stomach. I had also read that pure cocoa chocolate contained more antioxidants than green vegetables!

I watched, fascinated, as they drained every drop and began flexing their muscles and laughing. The goat's grease dribbled onto the stone floor and smelt like farmyard cheese. The servants dispersed and were replaced by others escorting young girls down the winding pathway. The girls were shy and seemed reluctant to be dispatched, while the men lasciviously eyed them with eager anticipation of ancient rites to be fulfilled. I didn't want to witness what I thought was going to happen and opened my eyes with a shudder. Momentarily I was cold and moved quickly into the bright sunshine. I shifted my focus to Alberto, seeing his lovely face in my mind and wanting the minutes to pass quickly, allowing myself to girlishly wallow in the new flush of romance.

I met Gordon and Ella meandering down toward the main arena and walked with them, telling them I was going to catch up with a guide I had met. Ella glanced sideways at me and stopped herself from saying what was on her mind. Gordon was quiet and paused to inspect a stone carving. The others from the group began to mingle further along by a small vendor's trolley. Alberto appeared from near a temple with his group and came across to me. His rugged, dark features enhanced by the whiteness of his smile made me nervous. I introduced him to Gordon and Ella, but we didn't have time to speak as he swept me along to the front of the queue and asked me what I wanted to drink. He took a can of Coke for himself and an orange juice for me out of the vendor's fridge, then taking my arm, he walked me away from the crowd. I heard Ella in the distance say to Gordon, "Do you think she'll be all right? Shall we go with her?"

Gordon gave a thoughtful response. "She can look after herself!"

We sat in an overgrown meadow away from the others. My heart was quickening, I felt he could hear it through the imposing birdsong. We drank our beverages and exchanged brief outlines of our lives. He spoke very good English and seemed extremely knowledgeable about his people's history. As I listened, he drew out of his pocket a large block of dark chocolate, explaining that theirs was the best in the world, made from special beans and that it was "good for energy." We ate some together. The smooth richness melted across my tongue. We kissed briefly, with the lingering taste of it coating our lips.

"Come, I want to show you something," he said, helping me up with his strong arm.

I held his hand as he led me toward a towering temple.

"Not many people see this!" he said softly.

He escorted me to a side entrance that led to a tunnel underneath the temple. I stopped, drawing in a sharp intake of breath.

"Don't worry!" he said coaxingly.

I wanted to believe him. He pulled my arm, taking me further into the tunnel, which wound around deeper down under ground. I stopped. I was afraid. He pounced on me with his passion, smothering me with kisses. Part of me was also hungry for love, but part of me was afraid, and I withdrew.

"Please, please let me," he pleaded, his harsh hands roaming everywhere.

I began to fight back.

"Let me take one pubic hair?"

I was shocked, and my anger fired strength to sharply push him away. He was caught off-balance for a moment, and I ran. He didn't chase after me. I was grateful for that. As I rushed out into the sunshine, the world was still the same, but for me everything had changed. I caught my breath and held onto the side of the temple. I wanted to cry. I had been so stupid! I was thinking romantically and he was lusting. I had to walk back calmly to the group and pretend all was fine. Ella knew as soon as she saw me and put her arm around my shoulder. We didn't have to speak.

The rest of the trek through the jungle was a blur. I felt that he was laughing at me. I must have been another silly woman who had been flattered by his attention. I just wanted to forget the incident, but when we returned to Flores, I was nervous. He knew where our party was staying and had said earlier that he would be going there in the evening. As Maria and I dressed, looking forward to another meal at the Blue Moon, I watched from the window to see if the street was clear and was relieved to find no one around. We enjoyed another lovely meal at the restaurant, but I still felt slightly uneasy in case Alberto appeared.

I knew he was around. I could feel his energy lingering somewhere in a corner, hiding under a street lamp, watching from a parked car, surveying us from the dark shadows by the tiny shops. I couldn't get him out of my mind as we ate. When we walked back to the hotel in the moonlight, I expected to see him standing by the lake, but all was quiet.

Later that night, I drifted into a deep sleep, a nightmare in which howler monkeys jumped out at me through a black curtain as I danced down a chocolate tunnel, dressed in a beautiful ball gown and falling down a deep crevice under a temple, where I was caught by Alberto. We danced through the jungle in a deep green sea arched by forgotten altar tables, suffocated by thick vines entwining their sinewy stems around our bodies forcing us into an unearthly embrace, crushing us into dust, which floated high on the wind, and we were lost forever.

15

Belize: Karaoke in the Jungle

Where is the now? In the classroom. The March winds beat against the windowpane. Grey day, grey mood, grey shadows pass through my head. The desks are empty and the quiet is a lie. The space only knows silence when it is not a classroom. The calm brings a sigh of relief from the constant battle, the chatter, the clatter of chairs, and the broken conversations deceitfully snatched behind bits of paper, and it's all a bit of a caper because the exams are too far away for them to care. I am locked, blocked in disillusion. I crave to escape again back to the journey, back to the newness of each day, even to the weariness and the uncertainty of the circumstances. The pile of unmarked books lie before me, and I daydream as I open the first, taking myself back to the jungle, back to the memory of Alberto, back to the hotel before we left for Belize . . .

I awoke early the next morning feeling more confident about myself, thinking that I wasn't yet left on the romance dung heap, for although the incident with Alberto was distasteful, it had a positive effect on my self -belief. I washed my hair and put on make up to face the day's journey to Belize. Maria noticed the change and commented on my appearance, teasingly enquiring if I was going to meet someone special that day.

Terrino, as usual, boarded the bus loaded with food for the journey. He explained that we had a long day ahead and that we had to have border permits ready, together with money to pay the various officials. Wearing my new aura, I felt I had ascended into a better zone. Everyone was in a good humour after the brief rest in Flores; even the Complainers were less critical. Bouncing along in our little bus, I noted the change in the terrain. It was so different from anything we had so far experienced. The rain-forest jungle brush diminished, forming into small agricultural farm holdings. We passed through compact villages where there were schools and children playing in the playgrounds or walking home, waving to us enthusiastically as we returned their welcome. The roads were a mere gesture, maintaining a basic connection from village to village. Poor Gordon's back suffered as we were hurled from one pothole to the next. His knuckles were white as he held on tight to try to alleviate the jarring. I promised to help him once we were in San Ignacio in Belize.

There was a happier atmosphere generally among the people, even though areas were poor. We saw women and children splashing in muddy pools, taking time to play in the sunshine; others playing football and basketball in makeshift play areas. The little farms were beautifully tended, and some had horses tethered outside. The landscape in some areas even resembled old rural England. There was an overriding sense of pride in the land, generating self-respect among the people. There were few cars, mostly horses and carts, but we did come across one single broken Land Rover whose occupants were struggling in the heat to replace a punctured tire. In Xun, the people looked different, with Afro-Caribbean features. Even the way they moved and went about their daily chores was alien to the province of Petan. There was a strong sense of community and peaceful ease among the settlements. We stopped briefly to refuel and were deafened momentarily by an incessant clicking of insects like the sound of a piece of paper stuck in a bicycle wheel.

Further on after the laboured ride we stopped to cross the Mopan River, where armed guards stood lazily watching the ferry crossing to and fro between the muddy banks. Large iguanas peeped at us through the long grass, and the biggest showed his disapproval by flaring his side gills and running up and down. I tried to photograph him, but it came out blurred. The river was a muddy brown flowing peacefully through the forest banks and winding its way through farmed mead-owlands. Alighting from the makeshift ferry with its ancient cranking handle, we walked to the Xunantunich Archaeologi-cal Reserve, where on the west side of El Castillo, a thirteen-story pyramid, there was an amazing frieze, more than nine feet high and thirty feet long long dating from between 800 and 900 AD. The beautiful carvings featured earth monsters, gods, dancers, and a three-dimensional image of a Mayan ruler. As I stood gazing at the scene, the rain began, and I took shelter in a grove of trees.

In a reflective moment under the secluded foliage, alone with the beating rain, a Chinese proverb came to mind: "If you do not change your direction, you are likely to end up where you are headed."

I felt I had already begun to alter the inner landscape of my mind. The meeting with Alberto had taken me a little further away from the pain of infidelity, realizing that in the whole score of things, it really wasn't important. True change takes place in the broiling inferno of the imagination, until it is soldered and moulded into the form of the present. I promised myself from that moment that I would never sink to empower those bitter thoughts from the past again.

The leaves, washed clean by the downpour, dripped gently onto my blue feet as a picture of Grandfather, a Mandarin sage, formed before me. He had first appeared when my second mar-riage was in shreds and my emotions were splattered over the bedroom wall, as I flopped with my chest concaved against the bed in a heap of battered debris. Grandfather stood elegantly before me in his long, beautifully embroidered gown, with his plaited white hair hanging in a pigtail over his left shoulder and his drooping, white moustache trailing past his chin. He wore a black pillbox hat and whispered words of comfort in a lovely fragrant garden by a lotus pond. He taught me many things. I could hear his words plainly: "There is always stillness before the dawn when you have a reason to cast off all burden; then not only can you see clearly in the light, but also in the dark!"

I remembered the bleakness of the black jungle and my fear.

"Fear is misdirected energy!" he had sighed, reminding me of an ancient saying: "When you go to the jungle, think of the shark; when you go to the sea, think of the lion; when you climb a mountain, think of a deer; and when you go to the forest, think of a rock."

I didn't always comprehend at first the teachings of Grandfather, but usually, the meaning filtered into my understanding later at some poignant point.

Grandfather had always taught his lessons with a quiet, mysterious air and a gentle force, which could shake acceptance of normal practice into insane disarray, guiding thought into a different channel. He helped me to do this when all kinds of unbelievable facts about my husband and his mistress came to light. He always appeared at unusual and unexpected moments, like in the forest, in the rain, in that moment when I was part of a harmonious vibration linked to the mind of the people past. Like in Palanque, in Tikal, the electricity of thought lies in the membranes of the fabric of the bricks, the earth, the air, the trees. In calming my own pulse, quietening my thoughts, I could connect with that universal quivering, the shivering of being.

I closed my eyes, feeling the vibration of the moment remembering an incredible event when I entered an altered state of reality. I was staying with a friend in West Sussex, England, during a time when I worked for part of the week in London. She got to know me very well and believed in my healing and psychic gifts, so much so that she sought my help to free a friend from an invasive spirit that had entered her life when she was nine years old. Seventeen years later, she was still its victim. It was peculiar that at the time it had entered her life I had a dream about her. I did not know her and had never visited West Sussex. The dream was horrendous, with an evil force that I never thought I would one day have to fight!

The night of the exorcism of that evil spirit had been long and eventful, and in order to undertake the dangerous operation, it had been necessary to encapsulate myself in a bubble of energy, a protective film of vibration, which enabled me to battle with the horrendous entity on a psychic level. I woke still half in the protective realm and slowly got out of bed. Her children were away, so there was no need to creep around. She was a single parent and was afraid of living alone, so she had every room in the house alarmed. There was no inch, nook, or cranny which wasn't bugged against an intruder. She had told me the alarm code, but I am not good at remembering numbers or dealing with buttons and switches. I opened my door as usual, went downstairs, began making coffee in the kitchen, strolled into the dining room to get my bag, went to the downstairs bathroom, and walked into the sitting room to take my coffee.

A few moments later as I sat quietly sipping hot coffee, the whole house reverberated with alarm bells from every corner. She had taken one foot outside her bedroom door. She ran downstairs to switch off the alarm system and stood before me quaking with shock.

"I thought you'd turned off the system!" she enquired, wide eyed with horror.

"I forgot it!" I shrugged.

"But how did you do it? How did you even step out of your bedroom without setting off the alarm?"

I looked blankly at her. She was suddenly very wary of me.

"You know how sensitive the whole system is. You couldn't possibly have got through it unless you were invisible!"

As soon as the words were spoken, I knew what had happened. The energy field I had entered had rendered me undetectable from the normal human vibration.

It took some time before she could accept what happened without viewing me as an alien, and even now we both find it strange and difficult to understand!

Back in the forest, I felt the vibration, the energy from the past, knowing that every single thing, person, being, insect, creature, flower is in constant harmony with the universe and, like a taut violin string that resonates through invisible chords, we are notes in the world symphony of time, never ending, without beginning, having always been and will be. Rain dripped onto my face, and I opened my eyes to the high sun trying to break through the cloud. Grandfather was smiling.

"How many lessons does it take? How many suns and moons will you hide? One day you will find the courage to shout what you know and have been taught without fear of ridicule, for there is none, only for the deaf!"

Grandfather's face slowly faded into the drenched cavern among the branches. There in the moment of forever, I left a promise to speak the truth of all I know.

As I emerged from my leafy hideaway, the others were gathering by the main temple. I felt that I had been given a mission. Maria smiled as she and Gunte hurried down the steep steps, playfully calling to each other. The rain had calmed to a gentle spray as we boarded the ferry back across the Mopan River to our waiting bus. Everyone was ready to settle down to our next stage of the journey heading toward the border to Belize.

When we arrived at the border office, it looked like a tin cattle auction shed, open at both ends with a fine breeze flowing through, offering great respite from the broiling heat. Wearing a thin T-shirt and jeans and carrying my rucksack on my back, my passport, papers, and money ready to hand the official, I strode toward the middle of the cattle shelter to a uniformed man who was very tall with deep-set African features, sitting at a desk. I smiled and handed him my passport.

"You are very convincing!" he said in a deep Caribbean tone.

I was surprised and uncertain as to what he meant, and shot him a quizzical glance. He explained, "Eden, like the garden, you are beautiful!"

I was overwhelmed by his kind comment. My new inward energy was taking effect and shining like a beacon outside!

Showered with unexpected praise, I walked tall into the bright sunshine and was shocked to see Alberto standing at the exit. He was the first person I saw in Belize as I stepped over the borderline. I smiled, embarrassed to see him. I confess that my heart skipped a few beats. He looked different, not as confident or sure of himself as before. In his station as a taxi driver he stood anxiously waiting. His demeanour was apologetic. He asked me in a quiet tone why I hadn't seen him in Flores. He told me he had waited for me at the hotel. I said I was sorry to have missed him, but we had gone out that evening as a party.

"I waited for over one hour to see you, to tell you sorry for what happened."

I was happy for his apology and simply replied, "Thank you."

He wanted to know where I was staying and where I was going, but in all truthfulness, I did not know. He shrugged with a defeated gesture and looked disappointed, but I knew he could easily find out where our party was staying. San Ignacio was a small place and, as a taxi driver, he would know the town extremely well. He looked forlorn with downcast eyes, and I wanted to kiss him but walked on toward the local bus, secretly hoping I would see him again.

The bus was full of Afro-Caribbean faces, so different from the people in Guatemala. Maria and I sat behind two lovely little girls who kept popping up from behind their seat and staring at us. Their black skin set against bright pink dresses and cerise ribbons in their neatly plaited hair was striking after the long, sleek hair styles of the Indian women. The little girls found us fascinating and kept wanting to touch our hands, so we played a game with them that entertained both them and us until we turned into the main square in San Ignacio.

It was late afternoon, and the heat was gradually abating as we collected our bags from the back of the bus. The town was so different from anywhere we had visited. There was an overriding sense of ease in a laid-back Caribbean way, yet with many armed African soldiers watching, there was an underlying feeling of malice, of hiding behind closed shutters. Although poverty lurked and hovered around each corner, there was a laissez-faire attitude masked with fun, evident in their walk and general attitude of laughing at life. There was a diverse blend of cultures in the small town, with Mayan, Mestizo, African, European, and Asian races, with Asian and Creole flavours breaking through the Spanish spoken by the locals who were selling their wares from open stalls.

As we slowly trudged through the town, I noticed how the people walked with a slow, easy gait that was quite different from the Guatemalan Indians, who moved with a quieter, shyer step. Here in Belize, they were not afraid to swing their hips with an open approach to life. We passed wooden houses devastated by a hurricane, yet people were still living there and coping almost lazily with the awful conditions. On the edge of the town, there was a plot of open grazing land used for selling locally grown food. In the last flare of the dying sun, the Saturday market traders were sluggishly packing away the leftover fruit and vegetables, which were cheap and not very fresh. We were hot and thirsty after the day's journey, and walking in the dry dust was tiring. The main road was well maintained, and the passing cars and trucks drove at an unusual pace, kicking up the dust in our faces.

Maria and I straggled at the back of our party and were alerted when the shout of "Snake!" was passed down the line. On the edge of the road, a snake had wriggled its way from the jungle path and reared up defiantly toward our party. It was injured, but still with its remaining breath it fought to strike. We gave it a wide berth and left it to die. There was a holiday atmosphere on the edge of the town, with a few upscale encampments where people could spend the weekend or take long breaks. The jungle was never far away, and nestling on the border of open brush was our camp, with beautiful, neat gardens and lovely jungle huts in all different shapes and sizes; some with thatched roofs, some round, and some square. Maria and I had a quaint, square, blue hut, like a miniature house on stilts, near Gunte and Terrino's, whose was of a similar style in bright yellow. Unfortunately for me, the geckos, lizards, and small iguanas lurking in the grass, taking refuge under the huts, were alarming. I scurried along the pathways neatly hewn from the grass in fear that one of the creatures would jump out at me. Similarly inside the hut, although it was clean, I was again overcome by my silly fear of creepy-crawlies and insects.

Maria wanted to go back into town to the bank and asked me to walk with her. There was time, as the group wasn't meeting to eat until seven, so I agreed. On the way out I met Ella, who told me that Gordon was suffering, and I promised her I would work on his back when I returned. She quizzed me about Alberto and was not pleased that he was waiting at the border; she viewed it suspiciously and told me to be careful. The walk back through the edge of town was pleasant. The snake lay motionless where we had left it, dried up and brown like the parched earth around it. I felt uneasy as we crossed over to the bank. An armed soldier accompanied us inside the cash-machine cubicle, which was air-conditioned and was freezing cold. It was strange to feel the chill on my arms after such a long time in the heat. I was relieved when Maria's transaction was complete to walk out into the warmth, and we found a clean café to rest for a while and have something to eat. The fresh tropical juice was refreshing and the tuna sandwich welcome as we sat back experiencing the new zone; we had travelled a long way together, and, though I had been determined not to take on a maternal role with her, I couldn't help it!

After our brief rest we sauntered back to our jungle camp. I went to Ella and Gordon's delightful little round, white hut with a thatched roof. Gordon was not well and lay on the bed, his face pale with pain. I knew I would have to take myself under in a deeper consciousness than before in order to create the intense energy that was needed. Ella sat on the end of her bed as I began my breathing. The hot tingling in my hands came quickly as I began to massage his back. I saw in my trance at the base of his spine a tangled mess of wires like the intricate workings of a computer; it was a scrambled mess of spaghetti intestines. I began to tug at them to free individual strands, but it only seemed to exacerbate the knots. I asked Ella for a knife or something sharp. She handed me a pair of nail scissors, and I set to work cutting at the snarled chaos.

Ella, who was also psychic, said she could see me taking out white strands from the base of Gordon's spine as he sank into a deep sleep unaware of what was happening. She also said that the treatment seemed logical, as Gordon was suffering from disorientation and a confusion about the direction of his life and I was guided to help disentangle some of his bewilderment and anxiety. Sometimes physical pain can be the manifestation of inward turmoil. I worked for an hour in a trance unravelling the mixed mess of threads knotted in the base of his nervous system. Gently he came round from his sleep with a rosy tinge in his cheeks and a smile across his lips. He thanked me and I left to get ready for our evening meal. Maria lay on the bed talking quickly in Italian to her boyfriend, and I had chance to take a shower. The bathroom was clean, but I couldn't get the idea of the creatures lurking under the hut out of my mind!

Evening came quickly as the local music drifted across the encampment. Saturday night fun had begun, and Maria and I danced around our hut to soul music blaring from the jungle wasteland. We bounced along the little pathways lit here and there with tiny lights toward the breakfast hut, which was an open-sided shed with a kitchen built next to it. It was clean and well maintained, and there was a vase of beautiful exotic flowers on one of the tables. There was a battered guitar in one corner, drums and maracas in another. As we gathered, there was a great party atmosphere, and Ella took a drum and began playing. Gordon, who was relieved from pain, looked peaceful and shook the maracas in time to Ella's beat. There was nothing left but for me to strum the guitar. For the first time since we had departed on the journey, I took a leading role and organised the group into a choir, even the Complainers were game and joined in, enthusiastically raising up their voices to sing "whim-a-way . . . "

"In the jungle, the mighty jungle, the lion sleeps tonight!"

Everyone knew the song, even Gunte, who joined in bouncing his shoulders in time to the beat. The little candle lamps flared occasionally when a slight, refreshing breeze wafted across the open shed, and our voices lifted into the new night out beyond the crickets and nocturnal creatures into the "the mighty jungle . . ."

Where is the now?

Bright, sunny, Sunday afternoon. It is late March and today it is spring. I am walking on the beach at Runswick Bay, on the Yorkshire coastline, past the moors to an unchanged seascape. My little puppy dog has never seen the sea before or padded along the damp shore. He loves it. So many new things to explore. The sun is high in a baby-blue sky, and the white candyfloss clouds sail over a playful sea. Today I feel the sun on my face and take time to sigh out across the ocean. The hazy film of routine lifts, and I can see again.

I embrace the warmth after a long, cold, dark winter of worry and pain. Financial worries still loom, but I am still here, still breathing, surviving. The operation on my knee has not been successful, and my continual pain is weighing me down. I have tried throughout the bitter winter to struggle teaching dance. I will not give in, yet I am afraid to return to the surgeon. Now the daffodils are in bloom, and I am sitting high above the beach watching the sea spray erupt against the slippery rocks. At the pub high on the hill, I sip mulled wine and watch the steam rise from the plum-red elixir, twisting out of the glass into the fresh open air. Runswick Bay, a place to remember. A place where my children played in the sand and my little baby boy fell down a rock pool, smothered in green slime from head to toe. A place where I had a fall before my little girl was born and had to be rushed to Scarborough Hospital. A place where I had the dream of the terrible evil force that I was later to fight.

Just before my fourth baby was born, I was staying in a caravan near a farmhouse and had a dreadful nightmare, which occurred several times during our stay. From the bottom of a large, straight stairway, I saw an open door leading into an attic bedroom. There was a young girl in bed. I was both the onlooker and the invader but somehow removed from the action. The horrific presence rushed up the stairs to the open door and the evil released in the room woke me in a cold-sweat panic. My whole body shook with fear at the sickening feeling of the attacker. I couldn't get it out of my head and had the same dream the next night and the next. I tried to forget it, but it only faded in time, and even then, it occasionally recurred, each time leaving me with the stench and disgust of undiluted malevolence.

Laying aside the memories, returning home from a beautiful day at the seaside with my tired puppy, I enter my garden full of spring flowers. When did it happen? Have I been so lost in my daily routine that I failed to notice my cherry tree full of pink, sweet blossom? When did the miniature daffodils peep through the cracks in the rockery, showering the white boulders in a coverlet of yellow? Where have I been? I sit under my beautiful old tree smothered in pink snow and watch my little dog bound around the lawn with sandy paws, pondering the depth to which I have unknowingly descended into a pit of depression, keeping my head down day after day enduring pain, working, sleeping, battering myself with the rigours of living. But today is a calm breath in a choppy sea, and I know I must return to myself, find my essence lost somewhere in a classroom. My mind draws up a vibration of happiness, a harmonious moment in the jungle in Belize, where spontaneously we had joined together in song,

"Wheyeee hep up boy, a-whim-a-way-a whim-a-way . . . !"

That evening our little group grew closer as we walked out to the town under the bright stars, with the edge of the jungle on our left, the desolated wooden houses on our right, and the dead snake still lying in a decaying heap on the path. Terrino led us to a massive outdoor restaurant where the smell of barbequed chicken and beef with fried onions wafted deliciously in the evening air. There was a great family atmosphere, everyone relaxing after the week's drudge, with children laughing, playing games, mothers gossiping with their friends and dads drinking beer with their mates. We all ordered assorted dishes and were amazed at the size of the portions— steaks hanging off the edges of large plates, roasted half chickens the size of whole ones, enough barbequed ribs to feed a large family, and tons of bread and salad. It was an amazing feast, after which we tumbled back to the camp, although Gordon, Terrino, and Gunte decided to party on into the small hours.

The next morning I awoke to the jungle cacophony outside my window and got ready for breakfast, jogging my way down to the shed through the dewy path in case an iguana shot out. In the enclosure, the owner and a small team were busy making full breakfasts. The smell of egg and bacon meandered through the tamed brush, inviting the rest of our party to eat. It was a joy to have a wholesome breakfast in the shade while being able to put my hand out through the open frame to touch the exotic plants in the garden hewn out of the jungle. Everyone had made plans for the day, and I, as usual, was left in camp. Ella, Gordon, and Gunte were to explore the amazing Actun Tunichil Muknal cave, which I did not have the courage to do, as part of the adventure meant going under water, but I would have loved to have witnessed one of the remaining untouched ritual quarters of the Maya, where the evidence of human sacrifice and torture still exists.

The day was quiet for me as I drifted lazily through some washing and had lunch at the previous night's restaurant, slept, and waited in the shade for the others to return. Maria appeared first from her canoeing trip and related how she had fallen in the water several times but had enjoyed the whole day. Ava and Henry came back in a taxi from an excursion to some famous waterfalls, but when Ella, Gordon, and Gunte returned, they appeared somewhat shocked. Back in their hut, Ella related the day's events to me, explaining how they had trekked by a river, crawled under a tunnel, waded through water, and climbed to the entrance of a cave, where "as soon as you entered the dark rock, you felt that something terrible had been there," she said. "Pots, pans, and the evidence of cooking utensils lay scattered on the ground as though something had disturbed the people and they had left in a hurry. It was just as they left it. It gave me an eerie feeling, all the ceremonial artefacts used for human sacrifice, with bones and skulls lying next to sharp blades and instruments of torture.

"Believe me it was evil. The Maya used the cave to make contact with their gods, but it was horrific. You could feel the terror of the victims from the dried blood-stained pots. Then we had to make our way through the cave's water system wearing helmets, and there was one tiny entrance that I didn't think Gordon or I were going to get through, but with a little pushing and pulling from the guide, we managed it. One of the most shocking things was climbing up into a small chamber where the skeleton of a young girl lay cramped up in a corner on a ledge with her legs splayed open as though she had been brutally raped and left to die. She had obviously run away, trying to hide from her torturer but was trapped. It was horrible! I tell you, I will never forget it!"

Neither will I. Although the picture was secondhand and I later saw Gunte's photographs, the absolute horror of dire evil haunts me, like when I first encountered the evil spirit who abused the young girl in my reoccurring nightmare . . .

I stayed at my friend Beth's house for a couple of nights each week in West Sussex, as my work demanded, and for her birthday I arranged to take her out for a meal in a nearby pub. As we sat talking she steered the conversation toward her friend Philippa, who at the age of nine had been the target for a horrendous attack. Her room, as I had dreamt it, was at the top of a large flight of stairs leading to an attic. As she told me about her friend, my dream returned in all its horror. The surrounding area in the pub where we sat went cold, and Beth said my face changed. It was not me and there was fire in my eyes and my voice came from another dimension. Beth was scared. I insisted on seeing Philippa after our meal, and as she tried to contact her, strange things began to happen to her mobile. We didn't waste time and drove straight to Philippa's house.

Staring into her adult eyes, I could see the face of the child at the top of the attic stairs whose terror had haunted me in my dream, on and off for seventeen years! I listened to her terrible story and, placing myself back into the dream, I could see her bedroom clearly and described all the things she had by her bed. She was amazed that I could see it and was shocked to remember back to when he had first stood in the doorway, his huge, dark frame shutting out the light from the stairs. As she recounted his first visit, I could see him with her, watch his dark eyes, and feel his evil intent. Information about him flooded into my head as we sat in her quiet lounge. He was a lay preacher. His name was John. In my dream I had followed him up the stairs and was always swept back by the wave of terror that engulfed me.

As I spoke his name out loud in the silence, the outside door blew open with a searing rush, rattling the windows, filling the room briefly with a violent cold, which brooded near her head. We screamed as the wind gushed and circled around before dissipating as quickly as it had entered. We sat dumbly for a few moments, afraid almost to breathe. We felt his evil presence. As I entered a trance state, I saw a little girl with blonde hair wandering around in a daze. She was in the kitchen of Philippa's old house. I asked her about the girl and she gasped. She said she often saw her but didn't know who she was, as no one else could see her.

"And the old woman in the chair by the fire, who is she?" I enquired.

Philippa looked at me, troubled.

"Well, only I saw her, except that I thought my father did, as he boarded up the fireplace and refused to use the space as a living room!"

I could see the old woman dressed plainly in grey, like her tortured soul, grey with worry, wracked with fear, afraid to speak the truth about her evil husband, John the Preacher!

"Can you help me?" she implored.

"Yes. I think that's why I had the dream about you all those years ago. He has not accepted his death and feeds off your body, sucking out your life blood!"

Poor Philippa was thin, gaunt, and pale. She nodded, but I knew that part of her had lived with his evil energy for most of her life and that she was almost afraid to be without him. Without her, he would have to face himself in his own hell, but while he had the power to keep her imprisoned, he was earthbound.

I urged Philippa to describe her torment. With a quiet acceptance, she related how he used to come to her room at night. She knew when he was about to enter, as her things by her bed used to shake. His force was too strong for her to fight, as he pushed her body down into the bed. She couldn't move or breathe until the physical assault was over.

"Does he physically assault you now?" I gently questioned.

"No, but his presence is disgusting and he doesn't leave me alone!"

I knew what had to be done, but it was going to be a terrible fight, and if I were to lose, I could be another victim! We had to have a safe, quiet place in which to engineer the ritual. Beth and Philippa exchanged glances.

"Shall I tell her?" asked Beth.

Philippa nodded.

"You see, Phil works as a, er, hostess for a man who owns a brothel, and she has the keys, and there's no one there on Wednesday nights!"

I was slightly shocked but agreed that it would be an ideal place.

"It's just an ordinary house" Philippa said with a shrug.

Back in the small, round hut in the jungle, I was a million years away from West Sussex, and I shuddered remembering the evil there, but I was brought out of my memory by Terrino knocking on the wooden door. Ella rose to let him in as he called out, "Come on, ladies, time to eat!"

We laughed as we followed him to meet the others assembled in the breakfast shed. He explained that we were going to a very cheap eating house, but it was good. The inexpensive place was a Chinese take-away with a difference, as it only sold fried food. The small take-away was at the top of a hill on the other side of town along a main road where the cars and motorbikes flashed through the highway. Inside it stank of pungent frying oil as the two people behind the counter tossed chicken and fish in the boiling batter. The smell invaded everything and hung under a smoky low ceiling, congealing the surfaces in a smear of grease. We lined up like schoolchildren with our trays and took our food outside into the night, where we ate with wooden forks on a rickety, dirty plastic table, watched by stray dogs whose eyes lit up neon red in the car headlights as the traffic passed, throwing up dust onto our fatty food!

The Complainers were especially dissatisfied with the evening's arrangements and disappeared to eat in a decent place. I wished that I had the money to do the same! To lighten our mood, Gordon had a great idea. The previous night he, Gunte, and Terrino had discovered a karaoke place in the middle of the jungle!

"Let's go there!" he urged.

The rest of the party seemed game, and I reluctantly tagged along. Karaoke was not my idea of fun on a Sunday evening, but I was curious to see it. We ambled back through the town centre, where the noise of the bars and the disco resounded past the open jungle scrubland to where the snake on the path had been squashed, with its intestines bleeding in the earth, proving a great meal for hundreds of tiny black insects—which was more than I could say for our evening repast!

"Down here, I think it's down here!" signalled Gordon.

We followed down a short path through the bushes. Beneath the forest trees was a flat concrete building with a corrugated tin roof. There were no windows or doors to speak of, just large, open gaps. The floor was bare earth on which trestle tables were set out in rows, with wooden benches to sit on. There was a kitchen where bottles of beer and lager were served, and a large fridge on which a television was perched that showed the video and words to the songs. Wires and cables filtered along the earthen floor into the kitchen, and a stand with a microphone was set in the middle at the front of the tables. There was a single lamp on a stand in the corner of the shed, which created a dim affect, although the light in the kitchen was bright and the television shot shadows into the gloom outside.

We paid a minimal cover, which seemed odd, as when my eyes became adjusted to the gloom, I could see lots of locals sitting on the open window ledges enjoying the show for free. No beverages other than beer and lager were sold, so I sat with Ella and Gordon while they perused the songbook. In the meantime a local got up and sang in the rich, soothing tones of Nat King Cole, "This old black magic has me in its spell, that old black magic that I know so well . . . "

I was mesmerized by the quality, sound, and ease in which the singer delivered the song. If I closed my eyes, it could have been the voice of Nat King Cole himself. It was incredible that in the middle of the Belize jungle, on a Sunday evening, we should be enthralled by a local singer. Next came other delights, such as Frank Sinatra crooning, "I did it my way!" Again the singer's intonation and voice were exactly Sinatra's! The people must have spent hours practising every little breath, pause, and nuance. Each time a singer took the microphone, there was a reverent hush which spread throughout the audience. Everyone was treated with the utmost respect; even Gordon, who attempted a pop song and was dreadfully out of tune all the way through, was enthusiastically applauded. Terrino gave an acceptable rendition of Queen's "I Want to Break Free." Gunte sang an English pop song but only managed a few words in English with a chorus of "aha . . . aha . . . !" every few lines. Ella wanted me to get up and perform, but I declined.

It was amazing how the poor people rejoiced in the music, creating a fantasy world inside a jungle setting while being part of a virtual-reality video, singing alongside famous artists, losing themselves in a dream. The video backing brought semi-sexual images of white women in scanty clothing, but the village men did not leer lasciviously at them; instead they looked respectfully at the ground and only returned their attention when the teasing had passed. We stayed until the trestle tables were full with the local community, and I watched sadly as a man in front of me struggled to find a few pence in his pocket to buy himself a beer. I wondered whether he had a family waiting to be fed at home, as did perhaps many of the other men there who for a brief while lived out their fantasies of being famous singers in the little karaoke paradise in the jungle.

The next morning we were off again on our travels, leaving behind the little jungle camp and the beautiful garden. Just as we were hitching our rucksacks onto our backs ready for the trek across town, the owner's daughter came to me. "I forgot to tell you," she smiled, "a man came looking for you, but he didn't leave a message!"

Lesley Ann Eden

I thanked her, knowing it was Alberto. Ella gave me a knowing look and patted me on the back, singing, "Let's hit the road,
Jack!" in gritty Karaoke style. We passed the snake trail, but
only a bloodstained patch remained, a small reminder that all
life is transitory, merely part of an inevitable cycle. While we
waited in the main square for the local bus to the Belize port, I
surreptitiously scoured the area for a familiar face. I didn't see
one and kept my gaze on a Cadillac car balanced on the top of
a restaurant roof. I took a photograph, feeling eyes from somewhere close staring. As the bus swung around the corner, it was
too late for good-byes or hellos; that moment in time had passed,
and I knew I would never see Alberto again.

16

Caye Caulker:
Dum Spiro Spero

While I breathe, I hope!

Where is the now?
On a train travelling to Bradford. It is a Friday in April, and the early morning sun is washing away the grey clouds. The English countryside rushes past as I sit sedately gazing out of the window while inwardly wanting to scream, "I am not in a classroom! I am not jostled in the corridors or bearing the brunt of scornful eyes! I do not have to elbow my way past smirking, quirky glares amid twitters of feline shivers in corners! I do not have to turn away from good-bye kisses from churlish angels with lippy lips and persuasive hips! I have escaped!'

I am being sent to the Bradford National Media Museum to attend a course after beginning a lunchtime film club for the pupils. I laugh at myself, excited at the prospect of travelling only an hour away from York; I, who has been used to a nomadic existence wandering across the world. Now pain is a constant reminder of my life as a dancer, but in my school the music takes me beyond myself as the children glide, twirl, turn, leap, I live through their dance and their hopes.

One day I will walk again without limping, and then I will know joy! I remind myself of the time I was asked to choreograph the church's history of the healing sanctuary at Walsingham and danced the main role in "Dum Spiro Spero," musing how the Catholic Church would frown upon my gift if it really knew my secret! But for now I am buzzing on a different vibration, rejoicing in a corseted liberty, remembering the days of sunshine and timelessness out on a tiny island in a tropical sea as the train rushes past the past sighing, "Let me be free . . . let me be free!"

As the bus swung out of the main square in San Ignacio, leaving behind the clucking and clicking of geckos, iguanas, and insects, I felt a pang of excitement. Each new town, fresh zone, different country had a flavour unique to itself. I was eager to experience life on a desert island, without main roads or cars, only sand buggies and bicycles. Caye Kaulker was going to be such a change from all the places we had visited and would give a tropical beach flavour to our expedition, away from the lush forests and dusty towns. Terrino had told us that the reef on Caye Kaulker is the second largest in the world, after Australia, with coral canyons, fantastic tropical fish, including manta rays, sharks, and barracudas, plus there would be a great opportunity for scuba diving and snorkelling.

The local bus trundled along, and Maria sat beside me embroiled in a teenage strop, but likewise with my own teenagers, I wasn't going to react and knew that she would soon come out of it. The ride was interrupted a short way along the main road by police who came to check the locals' papers. They took one person off the bus and didn't even ask for our passports. Watching the town disappear behind us, I noted how the terrain changed, reminding me of the large plantations in Louisiana. The driver steered the wheel in time to reggae music, shouting, "Hey, lady, don't you know song is a prayer?" I smiled in acknowledgment of his statement and enjoyed "Don't Worry, Be Happy," which blared out of the crackling speakers.

It didn't take long to reach the Belize docks, but I was disappointed by the dilapidated state of the houses, some of which were merely shanty shacks or chicken huts, with bright paint flaking and peeling in the heat. The general rundown feeling of the place was shocking and depressing, as I had read so much about it being a beautiful relic of colonialism. Perhaps it was there in another part of the city, but we were unfortunate not to see it. As we alighted from the bus, the dock was throbbing with the activity of men loading and unloading cargo from small boats. The smell of the sea and fresh fish hung on a cool breeze that wafted from the docking cove.

Inside the waiting area there was a shop where we could buy snacks. Terrino as usual was the first to stock up, and we had a while to wait for our boat. I felt the uneasy twinges of tummy trouble again, but I only had one tablet left to use in an emergency. Waiting in the small bay was a group of Rasta boys, crowding around one of their friends, an artist who was busy sketching a portrait of his friend. Ava, who was a gifted artist herself, took out her sketch pad, and the two began a competition to see who could sketch the other the fastest. A small crowd gathered, interested in the outcome, but they were both winners as they graciously handed each other their work as keepsakes.

Inside, the waiting area was dark, keeping out the glare of the bright sun on the sparkling sea. Little boats anchored next to us bobbed up and down, thrown around by the larger boats docking. Gordon seemed in good humour but looked funny wearing long shorts, socks with sandals, and a large sombrero he had bought in Cancun. Ella as always was pragmatic and quietly adapted to each new situation, while Maria, who still wasn't speaking to the Complainers, was grumpy and sat with her feet up on the bench looking bored and tired. Gunte was taking photographs of the boats, accompanied by Terrino, who munched on a tortilla. I sat quietly in a corner updating my diary while Henry stood watching the water. We were an odd group and, although we had journeyed far together, we still didn't gel as one unit.

Lesley Ann Eden

Eventually the boat arrived, and we scooped up our belongings and threw our bags in the hold. The sun was scorching,
and I chose to take cover under the awning. It was a small boat,
carrying about thirty people across to the island. The engine
revved and a surge of excitement bubbled as the waves bounced
when we picked up speed. It was great to be free from all the
dust and grime of inland. I felt a fresh, salty freedom, breathing
clear air as the spray cooled my face. Myriad hybrids of blues
and greens appeared on the horizon, merging into turquoise as
we cut through the foam. The half-hour boat ride was over too
soon! It was a chore heaving our bags from the hold in the searing heat, stepping onto the wooden jetty, which creaked as we
sauntered onto the sandy road. There was no beach, just sea and
the dusty street. We ambled into another world where time was
allowed to drift uncluttered by bleak office drudgery and circus-
like traffic parades. No one rushed or hurried to do anything;
everything was taken leisurely. It was too hot to pick up the pace
anyway, and the island did not belong to a strict routine of daily
labour. It dictated its own pulse, its own rhythm and harmony,
which blared out in reggae form from every bar and café. The
island belonged to the Rastafarian culture, and other styles of
music were not generally allowed except in the Spanish quarter,
where the Latino beat throbbed in defiance against the laid-back
blue beat.

We wearily trudged along the sandy main street, placing one
foot in front of the other in time to the hypnotic "choochi bacca,
choochi bacca" reggae high-hat cymbal that cut through the
sweltering mirage shimmering in the middle of the road. We were
relieved to stop at a beach café set out under a cluster of palm
trees, where we collapsed in front of the sea. A large Rastafarian
king wearing fluorescent sunglasses stood by his stall selling his
paintings, beads, and pottery, calling out a welcoming greeting
which we half-heartedly returned. Under the palm-thatched
roof, our parched party ordered drinks, drinks, and more drinks
before we ordered our barbequed lunch, which was cooked on
an open grill. There was an assortment of fish and steak served
with home-grown salad. A gentle breeze wafted carelessly over

142

our backs as we sat satiated after our meal, feeling too baked to move, but Terrino got us on down the main street to a sandy avenue, to our youth hostel type accommodation.

Inside we were met by a youthful, hippielike Englishman, Donovan, from Essex, who gave us a friendly welcome and showed us to our rooms. These were adequate and reasonably clean. Maria and I had got used to sharing, and we naturally fell into our usual routine of throwing our things onto our chosen beds. The small room was not air conditioned, and when we opened the window, unfortunately, the people next door could see directly into our bedroom! The short walk had made us sweat profusely, so we showered, taking care not to open the bathroom window.

Donovan and his wife had been on the island for seven years, but she had taken their small son for a break in Essex while he looked after guests. He explained that after the last terrible hurricane, the island had been badly damaged and had lost a small part of land at the end of the main road, which they called the Split. There was a good bar at the Split that served snacks, food, and great cocktails. Maria, who had stumbled out of her mood, decided to go with me to explore the Split and sample the drinks. It was lovely to wear a long, flowing skirt that flapped in the sea breeze and to hide from the intense heat under a floppy straw hat. It was holiday fun down at the Split with "I Shot the Sheriff" and other reggae music blaring out across the ramshackle bar. Everyone was there when we arrived and had made headway into the cocktails. Gordon bought me a concoction of white rum, coconut, and tropical fruit, which I adored!

As there was no beach, people lay out on the concrete jetty or dived into the sea from broken tree stumps, using the tiny inlet by the Split as a natural playground. Rastafarian young men played ball in the clear salt water, and their long locks cascaded into the blue depths like jet coral, splaying out under the water, pulsing like giant octopi. Young children paddled by the bar with a beef burger in one hand and a Coke in the other, laughing at the tiny fishes biting their feet. They invited me to paddle with them, and I walked gingerly into the cool cove—blue sandals, long skirt and all! The water was warm and refreshing, but the shoal of tiny fishes collecting around my ankles made me nervous as they nibbled the hairs on my legs. I stayed with the children for a few minutes enjoying their fun, but the heat overhead was too intense and the fishes too tickly.

I sat on the edge of the rickety bar drying off and enjoying another cocktail as I waited for the sun to dip below the azure horizon in a fiery blaze while the reggae throbbed on lethargically. The island pulsed soporific sensual rhythm as we sat under twinkling lights in the evening, waiting for our barbequed lobster served in plastic trays with a white bread roll and slippery butter. The owner of the seafront café was large, dishevelled, and greedy to make money. The meal was not very filling and was about as exciting as a girl guide jamboree! It was not the treat Terrino had made out it to be, so Maria and I trundled back to our tiny room to sleep in the sweltering heat of the night.

The next morning Maria and I had breakfast of fruit by the sea, but she didn't feel well so I took her back to the room to sleep, promising to collect her later. As I stepped out of the door, one of the young men who had been playing in the sea by the bar walked past. He was the tallest man on the island, from the Masi tribe and, true to his roots, could jump very high and was a champion at basketball. Jerimiah asked if I wanted to see around the island, but I wasn't sure!

"What you frightened of, lady?"

It wasn't that I was frightened, I was just nervous of the situation, but as I was going in the same direction, it seemed silly not to walk with him. He was polite and delighted to show me the layout of the island. He was proud that they were pretty much self-sufficient. "We got all de fruit trees, breadfruit, papaya, melon, sugarcane, coffee, plenty o' fish, and scrappy chickens!" he laughed.

He loved the plants and flowers and was a gardener across the Split, where they were building new houses. I admired a pretty flower and he plucked it for me.

"What is it called?" I asked him.

"I don't know what it called, but man, it grows everywhere!" he shrugged.

He showed me the large generator that supplied the island with electricity. It was encased in a wall by a clump of trees that had been decimated by the last hurricane. We ambled through rough ground littered with broken bottles, beer cans, and paper toward an old man mending lobster pots. It was not the island I had imagined ! Huddled near a group of caravans were broken washing machines and fridges abandoned in a wilderness of scrap. We paused near a dilapidated wooden hut with blue paint hanging off in strips. "You want a drink?" he enquired.

I nodded and followed him inside a makeshift shop. He ordered two fresh orange juices, which came in used plastic bottles.

"Do you want eat?" he asked.

I declined, and he ordered a toasted sandwich, which he munched as he continued the tour. The orange juice tasted good despite the container, and I thought it was a nice gesture of him to pay for it, seeing as he had very little money.

We meandered through an open playing field in the middle of the island, which I imagined was used as a cricket or football pitch. A small school was tucked in a corner of the arena, but there was no sign of life within the faded yellow walls. In the middle of the island was a bank and a few shops, a bakery and a laundry. There were some restaurants, various offices, and one or two luxurious hotels and private houses. But the island only consisted of a front street, a middle road, and a back lane. Anxiously I looked at my watch and told Jerimiah that I had to go back to see Maria, so we turned around and he kindly escorted me back. I thanked him, staring up into his wide face, and as I only came up to his ribcage, he bent down to say, "See you later!"

Maria was much better, so we decided to have lunch in a restaurant by the sea and ambled out in the rising heat. There were no customers in the restaurant and only one girl serving, who, like everyone else on the island, took her time doing anything! So our lunch panned out into a couple of hours and, by the time we had finished, we were ready to meet everyone down at the Split.

As we came out of the restaurant, Jerimiah was sitting on a plank waiting for me.

"What you doin', man?"

"Going to the Split. Do you want to come?"

He stood up lazily, nodded, and walked with us. No one said anything as we strolled in the sizzling heat. When we got to the bar, Jerimiah refused a drink and dived into the sea to play with the children. I bought Ella and Gordon a cocktail and caught up with the rest of the group to discuss taking a ride on the rum boat that evening. It was a trip organised for visitors which left at dusk, a tiny boat with a capacity for ten people at the most, where guests were served rum punch and small snacks on a cruise around the island that lasted until late evening. We all bought tickets, so the little boat was hired just for our group.

I watched the bartender slowly unpeel a banana for a cocktail. It was too hot to hurry; so I just sat back and allowed time to unzip itself in the lazy afternoon. It was too hot to think, so I only drank and drank more, soaking up the laid-back beat, feeling the heat, just relaxing, chilling. Time waited for time to catch up with itself in the lazy hours before dusk, and it was no use struggling against the moment; submission was all. Wallowing in the immersion of nothing and everything in the gentle calm of a hushed sigh, surrendering to a kiss and a lingering tenderness, pausing until the breeze returned, wafting black locks, falling in a soft shower around a smiling face as the afternoon adjusted itself, returning to the slow pulse of Caribbean time.

Dusk drifted upon us as we boarded the six o'clock rum boat. Two young men were busy chopping different fruits to place into the large bucket of rum. There was a light, happy mood as we sat on the edge of the boat dangling our feet in the water. Reggae music throbbed from the deck as we set off. The sun was just dipping beyond the hazy horizon. Small, white plastic cups of rum punch were handed out and were welcome; the fruity liquid soothed the back of my throat after the dry, sandy walk. Peace overcame the heat of the day and, together with the gentle evening breeze, lulled us into a magical ease. More rum punch and yet more rum punch glazed the night sky with silver lanterns, which seemed so close, I could reach up and blow one out! Dizzily the inky water blended with the black sky in one canopied velvet curtain.

My mind drifted beyond peaceful pleasure into a giddy fuzz, imagining myself gliding out beyond the galaxy, saying to myself, "When I stand before the Great Ones at the end of my final performance, the All-Knowing, All-Powerful, All-Encompassing will ask me, 'What did you do with your Songline?' I will reply, 'I danced along a vibration, breathing resonance into a step, creating the Dance forever!'"

"When did the Dance begin?"

"It always was, always will be."

"When did you learn the steps?"

"I have always moved since there was a break in the first star. This is my nature."

"I am starlight, I am golden, and I've got to get back to the garden . . . " I sang softly, hazily to myself as "No Woman, No Cry" jammed from the boat speakers. I have danced along the secret corridors of the Inner Temple and have heard the call winging through the universal grid of knowledge, calling, calling . . .

I began to cry. Not just a sob, not just a few trickling tears, but the full, chest-heaving, deep, roaring wailing, sobbing, screeching out to the night sky academy performance. Gordon, also inebriated, was sympathetic and downed more rum. I didn't know what had triggered my outburst, but it hurt my throat and made me cough. My self-pitying bawling nearly choked me and brought me back into a sober realm, where a feeling of utter embarrassment overwhelmed me, but I shouldn't have bothered because the others were just as drunk, and their singing drowned my caterwauling. They were too immersed in their own smoky world to notice.

Refusing another plastic cupful of liquor, I huddled my arms around myself against a chilly wind blowing off the sea. It had been a great ride, but out in the deep I was beginning to feel queasy. Fortunately we turned around and headed back. Everyone was jolly and needed help getting out of the bobbing boat when we moored. Most decided that they hadn't had enough rum and should continue their binge at the Split. I didn't want to indulge.

The quiet of the night hung softly like my tread through the sand. It was hot inland, and the calm breath of the breeze wafted from the bushes, sighing, whispering wishes remembered from the day. I did not see the eyes but knew the solitary gaze and chose not to follow. I turned my key in the lock of the glass door and entered the lobby, pausing momentarily before going to my room. As I entered, the heat hit me like a sizzling oven, roasting hot, ready for Yorkshire puddings! I lay on top of the bed in a cotton vest, my whole body bathed in sweat, my hair and scalp wet on the damp pillow. I couldn't sleep, but I managed a couple hours after Maria came in.

The next morning it was Maria's nineteenth birthday, and I woke her up with a melodic rendition of "Happy Birthday" and handed her a special card containing a present of lovely shell earrings I had bought from the Rasta king. She was surprised and thanked me. She and the rest of the party were going snorkelling that day along the reef and, according to Terrino, were in for a great treat exploring the coral caves and swimming with the tropical fish. I envied them but was afraid of the sea, since the time I was little when my head was held under cold running water so that I should know what it felt like to drown!

I was going for a leisurely stroll to take candid photographs of the less paradisiacal side of the island. I knew Jerimiah was working across from the strip and wouldn't be around to be my guide, which suited me better, as I could take my time lining up the shots. I walked the same route as the previous day noting more litter everywhere and was amused to see a huge sign saying BETTA NO LITTA, but underneath was strewn all kinds of debris thrown carelessly, dangerously, with broken glass, sharp wire and jagged metal sticking out precariously. Tropical birds under the archway of bushes bobbed peacefully at the water's edge. I found it strange not to have a beach gently leading into the sea, just a straight division, land then sea.

I ambled past the lobster cage maker's yard, where bits of wood, rope and yarn lay scattered in the straggly grass. Passing through the wood shavings, rats scrambled to the safety of their hiding places, making me shiver uneasily. I headed back to the broken track and toward the dilapidated makeshift shop, which was probably only meant for locals, but I decided to buy another bottle of fresh orange juice. When I entered the young girl from the previous day eyed me with suspicion and went in the back to get my order. She gave me a wry smile as I paid, which I returned as I walked out into the bright sunshine. I ambled into an area I had not previously visited. It resembled a gypsy camp, with pieces of cloth angled over bushes in a vague attempt to devise tents, and washing lines hanging across trees. But the strangest thing was the odd fridge and television plugged into a main line that had been dug into the ground. It was peculiar to have working appliances in the middle of the unkempt forestation. There was more litter in and around the camp. I felt like a spy stealthily snooping.

I turned around and there was a little boy playing by himself next to an abandoned washing machine with broken glass bottles and sharp shards of glass sticking out of the grimy sand. He was half naked and didn't have any shoes on his dirty feet. He had wandered alone from somewhere, but there was no one to be seen. I thought it best to move on through the bleak camp to another area where families lived in caravan-style accommodations of half-tin and half-wooden shacks.

As I passed I heard Latino music blaring from a radio and understood that the quarters belonged to the Spanish populace on the island. Round a corner near a copse, two tiny children played by a tree. They were half dressed, shoeless and stared at me, bewildered. A voice shouted from a nearby hut, and they ran away in fear of me.

Further down the track lay a dead, dry, dusty, giant crab sprawled across the path. I paused to take a photo of it as an old woman limped by carrying a large pot on her head. Through the next clearing I spied the verge of the middle street and made my way toward the bakery. Displayed in the window were veg-

149

etable pasties, and I bought two. The disgruntled lady behind the counter put them in a paper bag without saying anything. I wondered whether the shop was just for locals like the other one, as they viewed me with great suspicion. I turned down a side lane, which brought me back to the front street. This was definitely for visitors, and I spied a group of people sitting under an awning next to the sea. An old man from the group called to me, and I strolled across to him. He seemed to be some kind of guru, as people sat respectfully around him, but he was out of his head in booze and ganja, with empty gin bottles lying at his feet. He shook my hand and said that his name was Tobias, and the people around him laughed. He wanted me to join them, but I graciously declined and walked back down the street toward the hostel.

Near the cluster of shops, a man walked by wearing a red T-shirt and cut-off shorts. He carried a stick over his shoulder with three medium-size fish staked to the end. "Hello," he said cheerily, and I smiled, amazed at his fish.

"This for to eat today!" he said, beaming a wide African grin, his huge nostrils flaring.

"Did you catch them just now?"

" Oh, yes, every day is good catch!"

He came close, and I could smell his damp T-shirt.

"Where you goin'?"

Everyone always wanted to know what you were doing, where you were going, so I told him that I was going back to my hostel to collect a book and sit by the Split. There, Donovan was busy with mop, brush and bucket cleaning the rooms. He looked tired and greenish, pale. I thought it must be too much booze, ganja, and perhaps heroin, as everyone on the island seemed to rely on something to keep them in the "happy zone." Living on a tropical island was perhaps not the paradise it was made out to be! I had witnessed awful living conditions and great poverty, which kept people chained to the dream haven, sleepily droning on day after day in their reggae cocoon. In the meantime, I was glad to be part of the happy-go-lucky band soaking up the open-air existence on the beach. By the Split I bought one of my favourite tropical drinks and sat reading and making a few notes. Moments later the fisherman appeared and sat opposite at the cracked wooden table.

"What you doin'?"

"Reading."

"Is good book?"

"Yes!"

I really didn't want to be disturbed and, though he was a very nice person, I had looked forward to some time alone, so I carried on reading while he spoke about his life. He said he had been a policeman in Belize and his name was Jacob, but he was really a dancer and drummer. I became interested and put down my book. He said that he composed songs and accompanied himself on the drums. He also sang African folk songs and took part in many shows, as he was a member of the Belize Dance Company. I asked him to sing me a song. He smiled and sang a love song about a pumpkin and a watermelon. I clapped as a passing fellow fisherman passed making a comment. Jacob replied in their lingo and laughed, telling me what the man had said. "He said, 'Leave her alone, man, she's reading!' And I said, 'Well, she ain't gonna read all de day long!'"

But that was where he was wrong because that's what I intended to do. I sipped my bottled orange juice and continued to read. I offered him one of my pasties, which he declined.

"You know the old saying, 'No man is your enemy; no man is your friend; every man is your Teacher'?"

I looked at him, understanding the power of the spoken word. Silence hovered between us as the message rolled like the sea in that moment of infinity, crashing against the rocks on the jagged, broken land. I remembered another moment of infinity in a very different setting and allowed my mind to meander back.

I was twenty-four years old, full of joy and optimism as a newlywed, driving with my husband along the Scottish coastline in our brand-new yellow Lotus sports car with my little shitzu puppy nestling on my knee. It was lunchtime, and we decided to stop at a suitable place to eat. We drove into a beautiful cove, almost deserted, with a post office, a pub, and a few solitary cottages. The white stone alehouse looked clean and inviting set against a small outcrop of rocks and hills. My husband decided that we should take a brief stroll up one of the hills overlooking the inlet before lunch. The sun was shining hazily over the bay as we walked up the hill, and a flock of seagulls cawed, screeching a warning at us for invading their space. We paused for a moment as we watched them scoop and dive over the snow-white wash, surfing the rocky waves.

As we climbed higher, the wind grew colder and the thick grass sparse, interspersed with jagged rocks and boulders. A white vapour swirled, encompassing us in a veil of damp cloud as we neared the top. I shivered, unprepared for the complete change in climate. At the very top a cairn was erected, and my little puppy clawed at a stone near the bottom, trying to unearth something buried beneath. Just as I picked him up, I saw two figures sailing through the mist; one was a middle-aged man smartly dressed in tweed overcoat and deerstalker hat, which he doffed politely as he muttered a greeting. His wife looked pale. She was rather large and wore a raincoat and a pink paisley scarf tied tightly under her chin. She didn't say anything when I returned her husband's greeting. My own husband ambled over, and we spoke for a few moments about trivial matters. We then excused ourselves, as it was too cold to hang around, and as we set off I heard the man call out, "Remember, we're all Jock Thomas's bairns!"

I turned around to respond, seeing them hazily disappear in the swirling shroud. "What?" I shouted.

"Remember, we're all Jock Thomas's bairns!" echoed the reply from the dense cloud.

Inside the pub a young man was busy completing his morning chore of cleaning the bar. The smell of disinfectant mingling with beer and the tantalizing aroma of roast beef filled the small saloon. Although it was warm outside, a log fire smouldered in the hearth, and a lazy black cat stirred on a chair as the young man gave us a warm welcome. "What can I get you folks?" he asked in a soft Scots accent.

We gave him our order and as he poured the drinks I noticed a photograph behind the bar of the two people we had met on the top of the hill. They were wearing the same clothes.

"Look!" I said to my husband, "they're the people we met at the top!"

"Yes!" he laughed. "I expect they'll be joining us soon, it was so cold up there!"

The young bartender froze. "I'm sorry, what did you say?"

"Oh, just that we saw those two people at the top. We spoke to them for a while, but it was too cold!"

"Are you sure?"

"Yes, we're certain. In fact, the man shouted after us with a lovely message. He said, 'We're all Jock Thomas's bairns!' Wasn't that nice?"

The young man shook and his eyes filled with tears.

"Oh, I'm sorry," I sighed apologetically. "Is anything the matter?"

The young man wiped away a stray tear. "Those people were my parents. They owned this pub. They died in a car crash on this day last year, and my father always used to say, 'We're all Jock Thomas's bairns!'"

"We're all God's children!" was a lovely message delivered that day many years ago, and the crashing of the waves brought me back to Jacob and his sweet smile, when he had said we all learn from one another, that we are all teachers and everyone a pupil!

The memory faded as the sea behind me playfully crashed against the concrete jetty, throwing stray spray in my hair.

"Are you all right?" enquired Jacob softly.

"Yes, thanks, just a little tired!"

"I leave you to read then. Will you come and hear me play tonight?"

"Perhaps!"

"I play outside Mama Cass's restaurant. She don't let me inside, but she give me food!"

He stood up, momentarily blocking out the azure seascape, dancing a little jig and laughing. I watched him amble down the sandy road as I finished my juice and ate a pasty.

153

Later that afternoon back at the hostel, the others returned exhilarated from their day with the fishes. Poor Gordon had a striped red back because Ella had omitted to apply sunscreen, as she couldn't see without her glasses. Everyone had great tales about the colour of the coral, the amazing fishes they had swam next to and stroked, and the unbelievable caverns of underwater magic they had experienced. Maria was excited because our group had arranged a birthday meal at the only Italian restaurant on the island, and we were all to meet there later. As Maria prepared for her feast, I gave more healing to Gordon's back, which was red-raw in places.

Afterward I went for a walk. Out in the cool evening breeze, I meandered down the main street and turned into a side road, to the place where I had bought the pasties. Eyes watched from all quarters and, though the surveillance wasn't deliberately blatant, I knew that everyone knew that the English lady was walking alone. I didn't know where I was going, but the moon came out from behind a cloud and escorted me, just like old times when I was a child walking from my grandmother's house at one end of the village to my parents at the other. From a distance I heard voices and turned into a playground. I saw Jerimiah binding up his feet with bandages before putting on his worn old basketball shoes. I felt sorry for him. He pounced into action as the game sprang to life, and I watched him for a few moments before he spied me. We exchanged a look, a meaningful communication amidst a shot and, while his back was turned, I disappeared.

Further down the road I heard the heavy boom of the African drums, pulsing, cutting into the evening air. A voice bled through the intoxicating rhythm, luring me to a side street, where I found Jacob and a small boy sitting out beyond the restaurant. They sat by a fence with Jacob's drums gathered around them, and the little boy was shaking a rain stick. His sincere song plucked at the universe, reverberating out into multiverses beyond. I couldn't stay. I turned and walked slowly, his chanting tugging me back as the moon hid behind the cloud, mocking the scene; it's only a dream, it's already a memory, yet the voice echoes beyond the echo and always will.

We all gathered at the Italian restaurant and waited for Maria, who looked beautiful and was wearing the earrings I bought her. She was so happy and plunged into the celebrations with an alcoholic drink! The evening was lovely, although my mind drifted elsewhere, and by the time the birthday cake arrived, we were all quite merry. After the meal everyone went on to another bar, but I wasn't feeling too well and went back to the hostel.

The heat of the room blasted out as I opened the door, and my stomach twisted. I reached the bathroom in time to be sick in the sink. My head felt like it was being wrenched in two across my forehead. As I sat on the lavatory in the broiling heat, I knew I had been poisoned! The girl's smirk as she handed me the orange juice leered at me in the bathroom mirror. I guessed she was a close friend of Jerimiah's. The pasties handled with dirty hands completed the puzzle. I had been stupid, flaunting the travelling rules that I had upheld for years!

I couldn't move! My body was lathered in a hot-and-cold sweat. My eyes hurt from the inside and out. My throat was sore from retching; my mouth tasted like a dry dung heap; my head throbbed so hard, I thought I'd burst a blood vessel, and my guts were gurgling and churning! I stayed in the bathroom until Maria came back, but she was too merry to realize how ill I was and trundled quickly into bed, where she fell into a deep sleep. All night long I was either bent over the sink or huddled over the lavatory. I had been afraid of sickness; how was I going to manage the long haul from the island to Playa del Carmen? We had twelve solid hours of travel on local buses with borders to cross and countries to pass through. *Dum Spiro Spero*, "please help me, please . . . " I implored the Universe.

When morning came I was paralysed with an aching body. I struggled to lift myself off the bed to knock on Ella's door. She was shocked to see the state of me and helped me back to my room. Luckily I had packed the day before. Terrino looked very worried when he saw me and gave me a dehydration drink. Gordon ordered a bicycle taxi, as there was no way I could walk to the jetty to catch the boat. The others were quiet as they watched me lifted up onto the bike and carried out into the early morning sun into the sleepy street. I was so glad that there was no one around to see me. They laid me under a porch on the bare wooden boards by the sea to wait for the others. I didn't want to leave the island like a corpse! I didn't want to face the day in such agony. I took my last and only antibiotic tablet, together with the antidiarrhoea pill.

After a while the boat arrived, and Gordon and Gunte helped me into it. I sat next to Gordon with my head on his shoulder. I couldn't lift it to say good-bye. I just closed my eyes, dreading every bounce and bump of the boat on the waves. "Please, please don't let me be sick or disgrace myself, please . . . goodbye island . . . farewell to the song of the universe and the leaping prince . . . *Dum Spiro Spero.*

17

Nightmare Return

The boat ride across to Belize from Caye Caulker was agony; every wave that beat the bottom of the boat thumped my sore guts. I kept my eyes closed and knew that the only way to survive the day was to take myself under into a deep trance. As the boat ride was only half an hour, it wasn't feasible, so I endured the ride and took deep breaths of salty air. I was helped out of the boat and onto the jetty, and someone carried my things to the waiting room. I was too ill to open my eyes, so I sat with my head down until the local bus came. I clung to my little plastic bag containing my beautiful poncho. Boarding the bus, cold shivers rippled down my legs, and my head thumped feverishly. Terrino gave me more hydration drink, and I sipped it slowly, feeling the whole world closing around me in a dark vapour. I took out the lovely poncho, hand-woven of soft, thick, raw cotton, in black, grey, and white and imagined it to be a protective film encasing my body in a healing vibration. Inside my magic cloak it felt warm and comforting. I pictured myself wearing a black, round, deep-brimmed hat like the Mexican Indians, similar to my Indian guide, White Cloud, who had watched over me since I was a child. I began to breathe the breath of the sea, in for four counts, then out for four, which took me under, but not into a serene scene, into another nightmare. . . .

"It's a normal house!" Philippa stated.

Her words circled around my head. The brothel was a "normal" house in a wealthy district, and no one suspected. It was empty on Wednesday evenings, which was the day I always travelled to work in London and stayed at Beth's house.

I was going under, deeper. I felt Terrino standing by my side in the aisle asking Maria, who was sitting next to me by the window, if I was all right. She said that I was sleeping and that I would be okay. I felt Ella's eyes on me from across the aisle as I drifted back into the memory, feeling the bus jolt and shudder into action . . . taking me back, back, to a dark time, a different fight, another struggle for survival . . .

It was arranged that three weeks hence from our meeting I would perform a banishing ritual on Philippa to rid her of the terrible spirit that had abused her as a child and still clung to her, feeding off of her energy. It was the same spirit that I had dreamt about many years before I had even met Philippa, in an horrific recurring nightmare, which began at the foot of a flight of attic steps leading to a child's bedroom. I always woke up in a fright-panic before I could see what was happening, with a disgusting, overriding sense of fear and paralysis.

Three weeks was enough to make preparations for the dangerous ritual. It required long hours of meditation and writing out a set script for the three of us to perform. We needed special clothes, props, wine, candles, and other precious artefacts, which I would take with me on the day. During my first meditation I focused on the spirit. I saw him clearly. He was tall, gaunt, and gangly, with long arms and thin legs. His dark straight hair swept away from his face under his large black, round hat. His face was long, with a pointed nose, thin grey lips, heavy eyebrows and deep, dark eyes set in parched, wrinkly skin. His shoulders hunched forward slightly as he walked with wide, purposeful strides. His name was John Hardy and he was a lay minister. He preached in a large church not far from the house. His wife was a mouse of a creature, grey in every way with grey hair and hat, grey, withered features, and a grey coat. Their thirteen-year-old daughter, Charlotte, was quite different, with a fresh, English rose complexion, long blonde hair, shiny, ice-blue eyes, and an endearing smile.

I needed to talk to Phil about the descriptions to see if they were correct in her eyes, and over the phone she affirmed they were. I asked if she had ever seen Charlotte and her mother together, but she had not; she had only seen the mother weeping by the fire and the daughter floating in and around the kitchen, looking lost and lonely.

From my deep trance state, I was aware of the bus forging on and on through uneven ground, dipping in and out of potholes. But I never saw any of the terrain and only heard voices from afar keeping an eye on me. On and on the bus droned, taking me back . . . back.

My next meditation was fixed on Charlotte. She was a beautiful child in every way but was a prisoner in her own house. It was around 1865, when women were considered second-class citizens and should only busy themselves with family matters. Charlotte was not allowed to mix with any other children or attend school; instead she was tutored by her mother at home. Her father was strangely overprotective of her and made her hold his hand at all times when they were not at home. I followed her in her own little dream world, watching her play with her dolls and sing happily to herself. I saw her father enter her room, take her hand, and lead her out through the main door into the late afternoon sunlight toward the Church, while her mother watched them disappear from behind closed curtains.

I saw them enter the church and watched him diligently busy himself with artefacts on the altar, while she stood obediently by his side. He turned and looked down into her eyes and stroked her hair softly. A solitary candle flickered by the altar as one careful caress grew into several. Her eyes were puzzled as he traced the outline of her lovely lips with his grimy index finger. "Hush, child!" he whispered.

She pulled away from his fetid breath, but his hand caught her shoulder and held her still while his other hand slipped down to her young, soft breast. She tried to turn away. "You love your

Father, don't you? Surely you do?" he cooed. She wanted to cry. She was trapped. Suddenly a dark shadow crossed his face and he remembered where he was. He blamed the child for the incident and pushed her to one side as he completed the task at the altar. He walked toward the side entrance and bade her follow. Her heart was in turmoil and she couldn't escape.

The bus drew to a halt. Maria tapped my shoulder. "Are you all right?" she said softly. Through a dark tunnel I returned to the pain in my head and the sick taste in my mouth and opened my eyes. Everyone was getting off the bus. We needed our papers and money to cross the border. Gordon helped me down from the bus. My legs almost buckled beneath me. The air was hot. I was sweating. I took off my poncho. Terrino took my papers and money to deal with the officials while I sat, head down, eyes closed, fighting the rising sick in my stomach. A short while later we boarded another bus, and, with Maria by the window, I drifted back into the nightmare scene, reliving what I had seen in my vision . . .

John Hardy, a respected preacher, had a twisted sense of righteousness and was overzealous in his sermons, preaching hellfire and damnation to all sinners. Yet in his private life, he was cruel to his wife, making her life a torment and a misery. He loved his daughter with a perverted, covetous, lustful worship that veered from restrained desire to outraged disgust. In a moment of revulsion he ushered her out of the church into the bright sunlight toward a wooden shed at the bottom of the overgrown garden, where old, broken statues of the Virgin Mary and baby Jesus were stored, together with battered hymn books and torn organ music. He took the key out of his pocket and pushed her inside, saying," Now look, young lady, this sort of thing has got to stop!"

She had no idea what he was talking about and began to shake with fright. "You know what I mean."

She shook her head, tears welling.

"Now don't give me that, young lady; liars must be punished!"

He traced her lips with his grubby finger, bending down to taste her sweetness. His cracked lips bruised hers and she began to struggle. His hands clutched her throat, but she turned too quickly, snapping her neck from her spine like a dry twig in an autumn forest. She slumped to the floor softly like a rag doll carelessly thrown aside, her wide eyes staring up into the besmirched face of the Virgin Mary.

I watched his face change as he turned his back on her body. He inched toward an old green velvet curtain lying crumpled in a corner and threw it over the corpse. With detachment he took out the key, stepped into the clear afternoon, and locked the door.

Thirsty, I am so thirsty! The bus trundles on. My mouth is sickly dry. I take a small plastic bottle of Sprite out of my bag and sip it slowly. The terrain has changed from tended plantations in Belize to scrub jungle. Miles and miles of jungle forestation. Going back, going back . . .

After the vision of Charlotte's murder, I felt disgusted. "I know where she is buried!" I explained over the phone to Philippa. "When she was brutally murdered she was locked in shock and remained earthbound in your house. What you saw was Charlotte's spirit wandering in your kitchen. Sometimes when a person dies tragically they are unable to accept what has happened to them and they cling to the life they had and the place where they lived. What she needs is a loving funeral and to be given the chance to pass through the door into the next sphere."

My mind returned to the sad body in the hut. His wife knew when he returned alone, she knew what she had always feared had happened. She sat by the fireside and sobbed. When he alerted the police to his daughter's disappearance, she was silent. When he told them she had gone out of the church by herself while he attended to matters inside, she held her tongue. When he feigned misery and abject horror at his daughter's disappearance, she never blinked but held her gaze into the distance, sitting forlorn by the fire where she stayed locked in her sorrow, imprisoned in grief long after her own death.

"You had Charlotte's bedroom in the attic, Philippa, and that's why he came to you!" I sighed. "We have to not only banish him but set Charlotte to rest in peace."

161

Three weeks passed by quickly. I had a clear picture of him and his malevolence. I prepared the ceremony with utmost care and packed everything we needed. Beth was going to provide the wine and three single roses for Charlotte. Philippa was going to take us first to the house where it all began, and from there we would find the church. I was confident we would know her grave.

It was a warm October evening when we set out in Beth's car to visit the house of horror. I was nervous and anxious about the procedure and the outcome, but I had arranged with people in different parts of the country who had strong energy to direct their vibration toward me at a particular time and to chant a set phrase for ten minutes. When we finally stopped outside a house, my stomach flipped. I knew it was the one! I got out of the car and stared up at the attic window. My nightmare flooded back in all its terrifying detail. I held Philippa's hand. It was strange to think that all those years ago, pregnant with my fourth child, I should have the connection, should have the nightmare of the little girl abused in her bed by an evil force from hell. Standing there as the light dimmed, my anger bubbled and a hatred surged through me that was alien to my nature. "Come on, before it gets dark." I urged. "We've got to find the church!"

We drove to a street where Philippa remembered there being a church. It was a large, imposing building with gothic windows. We opened the front door and found a meeting for drug abusers under way. Although we were welcomed into the bosom of the group, we hastily retreated. We found a small underground shrine with a candle burning in one corner, but on closer inspection, an unkempt man with long hair and a beard rose up out of the dim cavern from a bed of rags and asked for money. Again we hastily retreated. "I know, there's another church, a smaller one further down!" Philippa said. We got in the car and drove two blocks away.

This church "felt" right. The light was just turning to a twilight glow as we entered the high gates. I went to the right, but Beth had an instinct to turn left. She was correct! By the side of the church further up was a small door, which I recognised from my vision. The ground was overgrown with weeds, nettles, and briars, making our passage difficult. I imagined the once beautifully kept rosebushes and neatly cut grass that led to the old shed.

Eventually after wading through long grass and knee-high weeds, we reached the end of the church garden wall where the remains of what might have been an old wooden shed lay scattered in unkempt piles, with grass growing between iron slats. Cross planks lay half buried as though the structure had been allowed to decay naturally through the century. We searched around the site and came across a mound overgrown with moss and grass. The shape and size dictated a grave that had been dug a long time ago. In our minds there was no doubt that we had found Charlotte's grave. I felt her presence. We stood in a triangle around the little plot holding our white roses in the closing light. We began the funeral verse in soft, gentle tones, lovingly applied with individual wishes, and as we paused, the sun exploded from a shaft in the sky, spotlighting the ground in a golden shower of beams, highlighting myriad dust particles pulsing in the haze. From nowhere a beautiful white butterfly appeared in the centre of the beam and flew down to the mound. The three of us hardly dared breathe. A silence stilled the air, transforming the moment in a haze of sacred peace. We placed the roses carefully on the mound and stood back. The butterfly that had rested on the grass for a few seconds flew up inside the centre of the ray and disappeared into the ether. In the emptiness of its passing, we wept.

Another bus, another border, another driver, another place, another moment of waking feeling sick. Another landscape, different people, another stop to get food. All I could do was to sip Sprite and suck a few boiled sweets, but the very thought and smell of food disgusted me. I was so disappointed not to be able to watch the scenery glide past and take a final look at all the places we had visited, but I could only survive by switching off from my body and riding out the worst, travelling back into the nightmare, back to the night of the ritual, back to the house, which was an ordinary house but was secretly used as a brothel, back to the house which would become a vortex of energy, leading to a doorway of the damned . . .

We drove to a well-established, middle-class neighbourhood to a respectable house, with its neat lawns and trimmed borders like any other in the avenue. There was obviously no one at home as it stood in darkness. We entered through the iron gates as though we were visiting friends, and Philippa unlocked the door and casually led us into the kitchen. Clean cups lay on the draining board; there was a cooker like any normal kitchen, but there was a sofa and magazines spread out on a coffee table, which gave a hint of a waiting room. "Do you want to see around?" asked Phil nervously.

Beth and I were both curious to see what a brothel looked like, so with schoolgirl anticipation, we looked in on each room. The bedrooms were clean and tidy, but there were all kinds of extras besides the double beds, which gave each room an almost clinical feel and an ambiance that was definitely not for rest or sleep!

The bathroom was the same, but the sitting room was normal, with comfortable chairs and a television.

We decided to perform the ritual in the sitting room and arranged the chairs so that we had a reasonable area to work in. Before we began I handed Beth and Phil the script we were going to follow and went through their responses. After the initial introduction, I explained that things would get tough and that Beth was not to let go of my hand under any circumstances. It was imperative to prevent me from being drawn out of the inner circle.

We dressed in special clothes, as our ordinary wear carried the energy of the day and it was necessary to work with clean power. Over our costumes we wore black cloaks. Mine was embroidered with meaningful symbols and images that would empower me with a magical force. We turned out the lights and lit candles at strategic points in the room. I had prepared music that would last for the duration of the ceremony. I checked my watch to time my connection with the others in different places around the country.

First it was important to cleanse the area with special water and then to create a circle of light. All the four quarters, North, South, East, and West, were acknowledged and their help sought, together with appropriate angelic spirits that would ensure our safety and return passage through the gates beyond existence.

With the initial cleansing, entreaties, and acknowledgments over, we drank the first red wine in ceremonial goblets. Philippa lay down in the centre of our sacred circle with her hands crossed over her chest. Beth held my hand. I asked Philippa, "Is it your first and final wish to banish the said spirit, John Hardy, from your existence, your life, your mind, your soul, from your being forever?"

"Yes!" she whispered.

I was not convinced. I asked her the questions again, and again she affirmed, this time with greater reassurance, but it was not enough. I screamed the questions at her, and she began to cry; I shook her, demanding her response, and she bawled back, "I do! I DO!"

I was satisfied. It was time to call the spirit, John Hardy, but there was no need, he was already there. He was not going to let go of his victim and placed himself between her and me. The candles flickered and almost died, dipping the room into bleak darkness; then they flared up, weaving a horrible shadow of the outline of a grotesque man. A smell of rotting cabbage, sewage, and disease filled the space. The air hung heavy with evil intent. Philippa froze in a coma. Beth and I heard him laugh, and her grip on my arm tightened. His face loomed in front of me, detached from his body. His eyes flared fire from dark pools of slime and sludge: he, the harbinger, the scavenger of disease, destroying with ease the ploys of the living, drawing all profound evil into existence, in that moment to strike. He clawed, gnawed at the core of my being, and my body shook. I screamed, roared, ranted, and raved as I tried to break free from Beth. I screamed a torrent of abuse at her and struggled against her strength. Out of my mouth poured words from a sewer rat, a cruel vat of depravity clogged up for over a century, released in an instant of defiance. The intense struggle raged, but I had great energy on my side, reinforced with pure sinews of power from the others who were chanting from afar, and I was further protected by my own outer case of spiritual energy sealed in a bubble around me.

The battle heightened and Philippa twisted and turned on the spot as though she were being torn apart from the inside out. With one final blow from deep within, I felt his disgusting weight lift, hovering momentarily outside my face. With another blast he tried to reenter but was pushed back, and a grey-brown blob shivered above Philippa as she shook and trembled. The putrid mass bubbled like acid devouring a body, leaving his head bulging out from the hideous bilge, slowly sucking his head inside. Beth and I watched as the gross features dissolved into the blistering cauldron, slithering away beyond the corner of the room out beyond the stratosphere, until the smell was gone and the room was washed in peace.

Philippa was quiet, and a lovely, serene glow encircled her face. Beth hugged me, and I apologised for the insults thrown at her, but she realised it wasn't really me! We woke Philippa, who had been out of her body, away from the violence, and remembered very little about the ceremony. She got up, feeling better, calmer, relieved from the invading presence that had tormented her life for a long time. She was free at last!

The bus trundled on and on in the gloaming rays of twilight. I hugged my poncho to my waist. I opened my eyes in the cool of the dying day feeling better. I had spent the whole journey re-living the nightmare in a fevered trance. Philippa was cured, and I felt that the worst of my sickness had passed. Recounting the fight against the depraved spirit had fired my own struggle against the poison in my body, and somehow the two had become one battle. Remembering Philippa's release filled me with renewed energy. I sat up with a clear head and watched the bus turn down a brightly lit avenue into Playa del Carmen bus station. I had made it!

18

Playa Del Carmen

Now is all we are . . . the rest is nowhere

The nightmare journey was over. As soon as the bus screeched to a halt, our party hurriedly collected luggage from the hold. All day someone had taken care of me, but on arriving at our final destination, things changed to a struggle to survive, every man for himself. Terrino led the group across the roads, through a thoroughfare, and across a main street to a shopping centre near the sea. I trotted behind everyone, struggling with my bags and trying to keep up. I was so weak and exhausted from the illness and the long haul. It had been a difficult last push, and everyone was relieved to arrive in Playa del Carmen.

In the closing darkness, Terrino escorted us to a small pub that had rooms to let, where Maria and I were shown to our last shared space. The room was as high as a barn with a white-washed ceiling and thatched roof. It was basic but clean. The bathroom, however, resembled a renovated outhouse. Maria let me have the larger bed in the centre while she had the smaller one near the window with the woven mat shutters. The corridors were open to the sky, with tropical trees and plants growing from a central vein, lusciously branching out along the passage-ways. Hammocks hung from posts along the walkways offering, alternate sleeping places if the nights grew claustrophobically hot. It was odd to think that we only had two nights left before our amazing tour ended. We had travelled incredible distances and shared a conglomeration of different rooms together; it was hard to imagine a night without wondering what time she would roll in!

After showering and changing, I felt much better able to face the world and took a stroll to the shops buzzing with visitors and nightlife. It was exciting to be in a lovely tourist beach town and a relief to have doctors on hand, as the infection and poison were still murmuring in my body. The shops were a wonderland of exotic Mexican handicraft emporiums amid a galaxy of different cafes and restaurants. Terrino had arranged our final supper in an unusual Thai restaurant, and as we strolled the streets for the last time, it was peculiar to think that soon, evening meals would be very different and I would only have myself to consider. It seemed a long time since we first met in Cancun. Outside the restaurant a life-size gold figure of Buddha welcomed us into a gigantic tree house with different levels hewn from dark wood. Inside were matching wooden tables and chairs with gilt Buddhas placed in strategic crevices. A central fountain calmly spouting water into a golden bowl of orange goldfish completed the peaceful ambiance.

I had saved enough money to enjoy a starter, as I, like the others, was tired of watching Terrino tuck into his and making everyone wait until the main course. I ordered a small hors d'oeuvre and a fish entree. The group was in good humour, relieved to have made the trip with all its highs and lows. The meal was lovely, beautifully cooked and served.

Afterward we went to a great café/bar, where live music shook the walls, hammering out wild guitar riffs across the beach. Out in the main street, we saw local Mayan men dressed in ceremonial costume performing some of their ritual folk dances, their blackened faces gleaming against their rippling, terra-cotta chests. Thunder exploded across the black sky as the tropical rain battled through the town, and once more my poor, damp, blue toes succumbed to the discomfort, beating time to the pulsing rock rhythm as the rain clattered out of time on the tin roof.

Later, back at the bar hostel, Maria sat stargazing at a young bartender and waved as I bade her goodnight. A fever began simmering as I made my way through the dimly lit corridors, where the tropical plants dripped, sagging heavily after the downpour. I snuggled under a single white sheet, afraid of what might drop from the ceiling onto my bed. My temperature rose dramatically in a fight against the remaining poison in my system. I drifted into an hallucinatory state of dreaming, waking, half-dreaming, not knowing what was real or hallucination. Someone was talking to me, making me repeat words, words which were planted on my lips, I could feel them, taste them, words which I needed to remember from someone standing over me. I couldn't see who it was but felt a presence; words, words I had to repeat until I knew them off by heart.

When I woke I saw through a crack in the ceiling a waving shadow of a single palm branch outlined on a white linen tablecloth. I reached for my pen and notepad and wrote what I was made to remember:

My head is as heavy as a revolution.
My body is as weak as a soldier's bayonet after battle,
But inside I am as strong as the person I am!

I did not understand what the words meant or who had made me record them with such passionate intent, making me memorise each with word with deliberation. The presence seemed masculine. I had no idea that it was an important message which would steer me later towards another amazing adventure.

As I sat up, I saw a greasy, waxy yellow substance on the sheets. During my fever I had sweated out the yellow poison from my body. I was embarrassed about the stains, but seeing the evidence made me realise that the worst had passed. I felt better and got up to shower while Maria, as usual, slept on. I found a café next door to the bar, as breakfast was not included, and drank three large cups of coffee. I began to feel normal again and relished the idea of being an ordinary tourist for the day, just lazing on the beautiful beach, watching the sea, being waited on, eating and drinking whatever I fancied whenever I fancied it! I needed to pamper myself after the harsh rigours of illness and travelling, so while the others organised their individual excursions, I selected my special spot on the beach near a beautiful restaurant with beachcomber huts embellished with thatched straw roofs, straggling long reeds dancing in the breeze like unkempt blonde hair. The fine white sand stretched for miles against an electric-blue sea, and as I piled on the sunscreen, a waiter came to take my order. It was sheer paradise! Although it was early morning, I ordered a tropical fruit cocktail with white rum and sat like a queen surveying the magnificent vista.

Over the horizon guitar players dressed in cowboy outfits complete with spurs waded their way through the sand ready to serenade the visitors. Small fishing boats bobbed playfully by a ramshackle wooden jetty as comic pelicans wobbled along the shore behind a little girl who was oblivious to their antics. A couple of pelicans landed on one of the small boats and stood like duo comedians in a night club poking fun at the workers. Various multicoloured seabirds breakfasted on the early morning catch, and the sand grew hotter as the sun rose. Just lazing away the time was all I needed to restore my health before the long haul back to my cottage in Yorkshire.

It seemed a lifetime ago since I had stood in the middle of my garden taking a last look at the flowers, wondering what was in store. A pang of excitement bolted through my mind with the realisation that I would soon be flying back to my little house, followed by the sobering thought that I would have to return back to school the very next day! I didn't want to consider that awful thought and resolved to immerse myself in the sunshine and exotic flavours of Mexico for the short time that remained.

I half closed my eyes and skimmed my view across the surface of the sea to the spot where the sky blended into the ocean. Squinting in this way, the world could be transformed and the ancient art of screeing put into practice to convert the world of the ordinary into the extraordinary. I was never taught how to scree, I always knew how to do it! But in the long-lost annals of time past, I have another life's memory of a little girl who was taught by a Blackfoot Indian chief to dowse for water, to scree for future information; to listen, see, and know the signs written on the ground, in the air, in the trees; also to love and respect the ancestors of long ago.

Screeing across the sea, blueness shimmered and the face of Chi Chengescuk, White Buffalo, Chief of the Blackfoot, hovered, his features forming perfectly as the beach faded. In the dreamy heat and softness of the moment, I allowed myself to drift into the memory of another lifetime, of a story as familiar to me as I am to myself. But I wasn't allowed to linger in the deep past, as the Complainers appeared and I courteously entered into conversation. They were not happy with Terrino abandoning us, as he and Gunte were going out that evening instead of spending it with the group. They suggested that we all meet up for a meal for the last time. I agreed and said that I would see them later back at the bar. They thought it would be a good idea to go to a well-known nightclub afterward. Agreeing, I wished them a lovely day as they waded through the soft sand carrying their sandals on their way to find more bargains to take home.

Left alone once more in the peaceful heat, I let the sound of the sea lapping against the shore wash over me and encompass me in the hypnotic swish and woosh of the rise and fall of the water. All was calm, serene at the end of the season with most of the tourists gone, leaving the restaurants and cafes in a quiet pause, tackling chores left untouched through the season, like cleaning roofs and taking down the top shelf of crockery. From where I lay I watched the cleaning scene from a detached, privileged perch, knowing that before long, I would be embroiled in routine and the quagmire of everyday living. I didn't want to think about the fears of getting across airports onto aeroplanes and through customs with the additional worry about the oncoming hurricane sweeping across America! But that was all part of the mystery of travel, not knowing whether heaven or hell waited, ready to pounce, if the night held fear or fun, if I would fall off the edge of the universe into a black hole.

171

Lying there in the idyllic paradise, I realised that I had abandoned routine to step off into the abyss of uncertainty, and I had expected travel to be a panacea for all my problems. But the reality was that they all still existed, waiting to be tackled in another zone. Very much like suicide! I had a message once from someone who had taken her own life. She needed to let everyone know that "nothing changes, only surroundings. You are what you are. Only you can solve your destiny; altering the sphere is not the answer, you still have everything to face and more . . ."

I gazed at the brilliant sky, feeling the passing of precious moments disintegrating all too quickly. I didn't want to return to domesticity; routine and loneliness tethering me to a persona that didn't fit, like an unfashionable dress worn out of a sense of duty to my budget! I sipped my cocktail, enjoying the tickling warmth of the rum coating the back of my throat. I wanted another, I *needed* another. Words from an old man filtered through my mind from a time when I used to work in Greece, a time when we would dance all night, a time when the old man beat his hand on the table, shouting above the party, "Why we gonna drink all night? Why we gonna dance all night? Because we gonna die . . . that's why!"

His message of "now is all we are and the rest is nowhere!" was powerful food for thought, which cannot be bought or seen or felt or touched but has to be lived each second within the microcosm of our being.

I ordered another cocktail, slipping into a realm of confident philosophical debate, inwardly arguing that, like words that fade and slide as soon as we given them birth in expression, they disappear. Life can slip away like whispered words falling on winter ground.

A fleck of silver caught my eye, flashing momentarily before it slipped inside a cloud, like a white shroud encasing a steel kite. I wanted to believe it was an extraterrestrial spaceship hovering, but the sun flickered across white wings that dipped and soared revealing a flock of birds ascending and the vision, a strange illusion, performed aerial acrobats across the beach landing by the fishing boats, not extraterrestrial, not even celestial but hungry seabirds.

The morning drifted lazily through to lunch, where I was served seafood on a wooden platter. From my luxurious lounger, shaded by my tropical umbrella, the world appeared stress free and manageable, without time restrictions and schedules, but like most things coveted, after a while they begin to pall, and I grew restless, deciding to go on a shopping spree. I had a little money left to buy presents for my children, and I went about the mission with great enthusiasm, wandering in and out of all the shops, exploring trinkets, jewelry, and bags. There was so much I wanted to buy but didn't have the money or room to carry. Down a side street I saw the Complainers buying a fantastic lamp made out of delicate shells and envied their purchases. They always managed to get the best bargains.

When I had completed my shopping, I sat in a café watching the tourists and the locals ambling through the placid pace of the afternoon. It was too hot to rush or get flushed by hassle. As I sipped my frothy latte, staring out at the largest cactus tree I had ever seen, with its dense thick branches and sharp prickles turned upward toward the sun, I noticed a skeleton sitting outside a theatrical shop. It was made out of wood painted white, with massive, dumpy feet with blue toes! It wore a gaily coloured waistcoat and large sunglasses. Behind it hung a gigantic puppet with a grotesque head displaying a set of angry, deformed teeth. At the skeleton's feet, winged clay cherubs posed naked with angelic smiles. Inside the shop was a cave of magical delights, with puppets, masks of every description, and theatrical clothing for all occasions. I lusted after so many theatrical props that I might use in my shows, but it was not possible to carry any, so I bought a beautiful, hand-woven hold-all to use for school.

Back at the hostel Maria was packing some of her things. I asked her if she wanted to come for the meal, but she had arranged to go out with the young barman later that night after he finished work. She was going to bed early to catch up on some sleep, then meet him later. I had already packed most things, but I unpacked them to use my new hold-all bag for my hand luggage. As I got dressed to celebrate the final night, I had mixed feelings. I was sad, but after the day's rest, I was ready to go back home. Romantically I had not found the great love of my life, but I had grown stronger inwardly, forgetting the pain of my last relationship. I lay in one of the hammocks along the corridor as Ella came out of her room, and we posed for a final photograph together, both sporting shiny, red, sunburnt faces.

Five of us met in the bar for our last meal together—Ella, Gordon, Ava, Henry, and I. As we walked out into dense humidity, the heavy atmosphere warned a brooding electric storm. The elements were mingling to concoct a special farewell storm. We reached an Italian restaurant before the sky was ripped apart with massive pink streaks of fork lightning and pounding rolls of ear-bursting thunder. The meal was quite pleasant, but I began to feel like breaking out of myself. Throughout the whole of the trip, I had sat back and listened to everyone speak, deliberately not airing my own thoughts, but with the trip about to close, feeling stronger, I was tired of playing the Miss Nice role and asserted myself, airing my views, which took everyone by surprise. Perhaps I was not the quiet, acquiescing person they thought they knew! Ella was shocked at my outburst of opinion and viewed me with concern. Maybe it was the aftermath of my illness that had sent me stir crazy after my ordeal.

After the meal we walked out into torrential rain (which had become an integral part of daily existence, dry feet being something I had forgotten) to make our way to the nightclub. The walk was long, tedious, and uncomfortable as none of us had umbrellas or coats and were completely drenched by the time we reached the closed doors. It didn't open until late, so we had to face the long trek back. Ava and Henry managed to flag down a taxi to take them to a bar, but I wanted to get back to the hostel. Gordon was kind to walk with me, but Ella didn't like the new me and hung back demanding Gordon walk with her. I didn't care! I was wet, I had a little money left, I had regained my health, and in a few hours, I would be making the long haul back home. I wanted to do Gene Kelly's "Singin' in the Rain" under a street lamp, but there were too many Friday night teenagers out on the town and, although my newfound strength gave me confidence, I didn't feel strong enough to arouse the attention of youngsters out on the rampage.

Back at the hostel, I didn't go to my room as I knew Maria was sleeping, preparing for her last night dancing with the young bartender. Instead I sat at the bar with glistening face, soaking-wet hair and clothes sticking to me like a second skin. The bar was only just under shelter, and if I inched a little too far back, the rain would drench my back. Inside the little drinking haven, the atmosphere was jolly, with the locals enjoying their Friday night fiesta. Inside the saloon, little wooden boxes were attached to the walls, all different, with individual markings depicting ownership, housing the person's favourite tipple.

As I sat sipping a large whiskey and Sprite, the Complainers came in with Gordon, who was a regular at the bar wherever we were. I bought him a drink in return for the many he had bought me and offered one to the Complainers. They declined, thanking me, as they knew I hadn't much money and told me graciously to spend it on myself. In that moment I saw them in a different light. I was sorry to have judged them harshly and strangely envied their ability to complain, as in many cases they were right. The trip could have been greatly improved with more efficient organisation from Terrino, but most of us weakly ambled along, not wishing to upset anyone.

Sitting at the bar I was empowered with a new sense of confidence. I spied a very handsome man sitting opposite me at the other end of the bar, and I shamelessly indulged in flirting. In that moment he seemed to be everything I had been searching for, with his large, dark, expressive eyes brimming with passion and zest for life; sleek black hair with manly shoulders. He was well dressed, middle-aged and returned my cheeky advances with a sense of playfulness. He hooked his index finger at me and beckoned me to join him, but I feigned indifference and indicated that he should come to me. I was brazen, daring myself to dare beyond measure. I didn't care that I looked a mess, completely soaked to the skin, with wet hair curling into ringlets. For all I knew my mascara was running in rivulets down my nose, but I didn't give a damn. For the first time in a long time, I was having extreme fun. I had nothing to lose. But what a blow from the gods, what dastardly twist, to meet a man of my dreams on my last night?

As he slinked off his stool, I dreaded disappointment. What if he didn't meet my expectations? What if he was a maniac? But when he sauntered teasingly to my side, I was not displeased. He was debonair, suave, and genteel. We kissed without introduction, like lovers meeting for dinner. It was so natural, so sweet. He spoke excellent English, with a strong, rugged accent, and I tried not to swoon, coolly introducing him to Gordon, who with fatherly interest asked about his work. He spoke to Gordon like a prospective boyfriend talking about his business as a graphic designer, but he had fallen on hard times, spending money on a divorce and was working as a waiter. He was interested in deep-sea diving and hoped one day to go to South Africa to dive.

We drank together, laughing, soaking up each other's energy, kissing, whispering, touching, wrapped in our ecstasy of meeting, avoiding the agony of the reality of the separation to come. We were oblivious to the raging storm, as lights flickered, pausing briefly before plunging the whole city into blackness, leaving us holding each other softly in the dark until the bar rose back to life under the cosy glow of candlelight. The wind howled, screeching down the street, overturning dustbins, rolling litter into shop corners while he held me close to his chest, his eyes never leaving mine. I had a vision of the winds of time sweeping over our bones that lay side-by-side somewhere in the rain forest. Our connection was too deep not to have known each other before. He felt it, I knew it, but like star-crossed lovers, we understood that our brief window in time was only a shadow of the past.

He asked me if I wanted to make love by the beach in the eye of the storm, but it was the last thing I wanted. I was content to have our sweet dream for a short while. Of course in the heat of the moment and the alcohol-drenched kisses we fought to find a way to be together, maybe he could go to England, perhaps I could live in Playa? It was easier to encase ourselves in a bubble of make-believe to cope with the pain of leaving each other. I had to be sensible and tear myself away from the Cinderella magic, as I needed to go to bed to get an early start next morning to meet my taxi taking me to the airport. He understood and was thoughtful and kind, insisting on taking me to the local supermarket to buy matches and candles for my room, knowing the electricity would be off for the duration of the night.

As we walked out of the bar hand-in-hand and through the pouring rain, we didn't need umbrellas or coats, we had each other. People looked at us as they passed from under their brollies and smiled. People beeped their horns in their cars as we kissed in the rain. Police waved and smiled as we hurried across the road; we owned the world briefly, not heeding the pain of needing. The intensity of the time shared was all, understanding "now is all we are, the rest is nowhere."

19

Fire in My Hands

*When the Great Ones ask, I will say I have
Danced my Songline, twirling and turning in
the ecstasy of bright lights, leaping beyond the
limelight, out to the faint melody of the stringed
universe, which sings only for those who dance
in the rain . . .*

—*L.A. Eden*

The now is summer, having navigated my way through a long,
dark, winter's tunnel into the brighter, lighter days of June.
Nearing the end of a long, exhausting school year, I wait for a new
adventure to unfold. I am sitting in my classroom with summer
sunlight gleaming over the lime-green trees in the quad. My exam
class has left, only their books remain. A postcard from one of
the worst boys is left where he purposefully placed it, high out of
reach above my whiteboard, his words still hang in the air: "You'll
remember me forever, Miss." Perhaps, but for the wrong reasons.

Another year gone, and the rows of desks wait for the next
batch. Two years of their lives and mine thrown together in
struggle, laughter, tears, and a sharing of ideas. I sigh, as time
has not diminished my stress of the tax investigation, which is

dragging on and on. One day I will find my little blue fishes, but until then, I bounce from fear to indifference, assured that I will not die in the process. Birds incessantly chatter outside my window as my new students roll in, too weary to concentrate, and the battle of wills begins.

> *My head is a heavy as a revolution.*
> *My body is as weak as a soldier's bayonet after battle,*
> *But inside I am as strong as the person I am!*

Words from Playa del Carmen circle round and round in my brain. Revolutionary images of Che Guevara pan in and out of my mind while the Cuban beat pulses, secretly, intoxicatingly, inciting ideas of hot nights in Havana.

"Sit down! Shut up!" I bellow. I have to win the classroom war if I am to survive and teach the exam curriculum.

We are out on different planets: they with their sly glances at hidden mobiles under their desks, their pens flicking, nicking pieces of elastic and plastic tubing to wave when my back is turned; me with my head in Shakespeare's sonnets. I want to escape but grit my teeth, only another half hour to go in the heat and the droning. But when the sharp bell shrieks. they rise, their energy and enthusiasm returning like a quick blood transfusion restoring life to the dead.

Restoring life to the dead . . .

I remember the face of my little girl, just four years old. I had left her with her grandmother to play in the park while I went to visit a dying man to give him some comfort. He was dying, not dying, just leaving the earth while his wife and son fought by his bedside to keep him anchored to the dull pulse of living, of pain, of sickness and confusion. In their love and anguish, they fought a lost battle. Energy, heat rose up through my hands to relieve his sickness, affording him a little comfort. As I left, the energy stayed with me as I drove back to collect my little girl.

When she saw me, she ran to me and, hugging my legs, pulled out of her grubby pocket a squashed butterfly. "I caught this for you," she beamed, "but I think it's dead."

I took the butterfly in the palm of my hand. Its wings were squashed. A dusting of yellow pollen fell lightly from its back. My daughter's face was serious. The energy was still buzzing inside me, and I concentrated hard injecting the tiny creature with the pure electricity tingling through my veins. My daughter watched closely. Gently there was a soft movement from its body, almost a ripple pulsed, but it stopped. Then its crushed wings opened. My daughter gasped. It stayed poised as though dazed. The wings flickered momentarily before softly beating, then it flew to a flower. We watched in awe, amazed as it fluttered around our heads before fleeing somewhere over the wall.

"It said thank you, Mummy," she whispered as she skipped back to her toys as though our experience was the most natural thing in the world. For her it was, as she had always known the healing touch. It was part of our life as a family with her brother and two sisters living the truth of energy vibration.

As the class pile out noisily, I smile to myself and pack away folders into my filing cabinet, remembering when my second daughter was at the school, just thirteen years old. I received a call saying she had been badly injured in a woodwork class and had been taken back home. I rushed there to see that her eye had been cut by a piece of plastic. My eldest daughter was with her and had ordered a taxi to take her to the hospital.

"Hold still!" I urged, taking her by the shoulders.

"What are you doing?" she cried.

"I'm going to make it better, now hold still."

She obeyed, gingerly allowing me to touch her eye.

"There!" I said, relieved to see that her eye was better.

"Oh, Mum, what have you done, now I'm going to look stupid. There's nothing there, it's better!" she wailed.

My eldest daughter laughed. She knew I would heal her sister. The ungrateful outcry was typical of a teenager afraid of appearing to make a fuss over nothing. Thankfully it was nothing, and when the nurse at the hospital proclaimed her better she looked sideways and kissed me!

Silence descends in the classroom and an unnatural quiet pervades. I do not rush to go home to my lonely cottage. I walk slowly to my car, spying a little grey squirrel darting up a tree and wondering about the lifespan of the creatures. Whole families of squirrels must have survived since my children had been at the school. Voices echo from the tennis courts and I remember my eldest daughter in her sports shorts coming home with a broken finger after playing netball. She was distressed because she had a piano exam that week. With the healing touch I coaxed the finger back to strength, and by the next day it was better, enabling her to take her piano exam, which she passed with merit.

My children have inherited the gift. For them, it is a way of life and something they always took for granted, like the time my son had an accident with a mirror that accidentally smashed across his leg. I was twenty-five miles away when I received the call, and while driving in the car to reach him, I began visualising his leg and healing the tear. I found him lying on the attic floor with pieces of glass strewn all around him. I worked on his leg, encouraging the rising heat in my hands to seal the torn pieces of skin. Before long the cut had healed and the bleeding had stopped.

There were times when my children were very young that healing was used instantaneously, almost routinely, especially when it was imperative to use mind over matter. Such a moment came when my children were at breakfast, the youngest sitting in her high chair banging her spoon on the table, my son crying because his sister had taken all the milk, and my eldest daughter complaining because I needed her to babysit. I was hurrying because I had a special assignment for the newspaper as a columnist. The kettle had just boiled and instead of pouring the boiling water into the coffee jug, I tipped it straight over my right hand. There was silence from the children. There wasn't time to rush to hospital, so I immediately denied the burn, using my inner strength to heal the stinging. Everything happened in a matter of seconds, and my skin wasn't even red. The children after a moment's concern went on noisily arguing when they knew I was fine. However, I forgot to work on the insides of my fingers, which were burnt, but that was nothing in comparison to what might have been!

For many years I denied my healing energy outside my family, but occasionally allowing it to slip to help children in my dance school; eventually after running away from it, I succumbed and secretly helped many sick children. Those who received help never divulged the source of their healing, only passed it on when the need arose. Now, I am not afraid to share the truth.

Where is the now?

I have just finished a dance class in my own school. I smile as I watch the students with bright red faces and shiny shoulders wave good-bye. I am so proud of their achievements and envy their physical prowess, as my own skills have diminished in a haze of pain. One day I will dance again. Sometimes it is so hard not to throw myself into the dance when I hear the music, but my leg holds me captive to the spot. I turn to put my music away and hear the door open across the studio. A student's mother sidles in holding a small box. With loving eyes she hands it to me and says, "This is for believing in my children . . . "

I am moved. Inside is a small pendant she had specially made and inscribed with *Life is not about waiting for the storm to pass. It is about dancing in the rain.*

Stray tears of joy cloud my eyes as I watch her leave the studio. Through the high windows the light bleeds into twilight hue, marking shadows lurking in the corridor. I lock up. I put away my music. The first star appears in the cool evening. I clutch the pendant. *Life is not about waiting for the storm to pass. It is about dancing in the rain.*

I remember the rain . . . I remember the tropical rain . . . I remember the storm in Playa del Carmen. I see my blue feet, my drenched body standing under a tree locked in his arms.

I remember returning to the room and lighting my candles. I remember Maria's hurt face and her body wreaking of cigarettes.

"Did you go dancing like he promised?"

"No."

I understood. I had played that scene myself and knew how she felt. Her crumpled body said it all as she fell into bed.

The last candle flickered and died, leaving us in the dim light of dawn streaking across a new day. "I have to go," I whispered, swallowing emotion.

"You are going now?" she asked, holding out her arms like a small child for a good-night hug.

I kissed her cheek. There was nothing I could say. We had shared so much, and it was time for me to walk out into the fresh morning air.

There was quiet in the street after the storm, with pink light glowing from the rising sun across the calm sea. The tree which had sheltered a newfound passion stood motionless and ordinary. The traffic light which had flashed a neon finale for a lover's embrace was dull and commonplace. The shop where two policemen had stood smiling at our prolonged good-byes was shut and its façade looked worn, lacklustre. Nothing held the magic of the night, only inside my heart was a memory. A memory of a lovely man who loved me for a moment and held me close, taking my hands in his, hugging them to his chest, whispering: "YOU HAVE FIRE IN YOUR HANDS!"

ADDENDUM

Whilst in a poisoned fever in Playa del Carmen, Lesley Ann was made to memorise a message from an unidentified spirit. At the time the meaning was not clear, but on returning home she began to glimmer clues which she needed to follow in a new adventure. Her amazing, true encounters with the paranormal are unbelievable, as her journey across Cuba in search of the authentic Cubanismo music and dance leads her into realms beyond imagination. Follow her next expedition where she reveals secrets from the lost Palace of Knossos and many other incredible revelations in her extraordinary account of "Beyond Belief..."

Lightning Source UK Ltd.
Milton Keynes UK
12 June 2010

155475UK00001B/6/P